An Introduction to Twentie

NEW READINGS
Introductions to European Literature and Culture
Series editor: Nicholas Hammond

An Introduction to Twentieth-Century French Literature

Victoria Best

Duckworth

First published in 2002 by
Gerald Duckworth & Co. Ltd.
61 Frith Street, London W1D 3JL
Tel: 020 7434 4242
Fax: 020 7434 4420
inquiries@duckworth-publishers.co.uk
www.ducknet.co.uk

A catalogue record for this book is available
from the British Library

ISBN 0 7156 3166 7

All translations are by the author, with the exception of
Robert Desnos's 'Élégant cantique de Salomé Salomon' and
Francis Picabia's 'Délicieux', both taken from *The Shaping of Modern
French Poetry* by Roger Little (Carcanet Press: 1995).

Typeset by Derek Doyle & Associates, Liverpool
Printed and bound in Great Britain by Booksprint

Contents

Acknowledgements

I am so grateful to Nick Hammond for letting me loose on this book in the first place. Without his determined efforts it may never have reached publication, so I am deeply in his debt. Equally unreserved and heartfelt thanks to Kathryn Robson, who read each chapter with exactly the right amounts of criticism and encouragement, and whose help in the closing stages was invaluable, and also to Elizabeth Fraser, another reader who provided a much-needed perspective. I am also grateful to Deborah Blake at Duckworth for her patience and efficiency. Much of this book was written while away; thanks and love to my parents for Bath, Stephen and Dawn Oliver for Aldeburgh, Jean and Dan Goyder for Brittany and Julian and April Best for Aldeburgh again. Much love also to Alexander whose health and happiness over an entire spring and summer made his mother's life so much easier. Finally I would like to thank all the students of twentieth-century French literature at Cambridge University who have been supervised by me over the past six years. Their enthusiasm, engagement and insight continues to make it all worthwhile.

This book is dedicated with love to my husband, Andrew Goyder, for being the best distraction from work I know.

Victoria Best
Cambridge February 2002

Introduction

Writing and Life

In 1994 Jorge Semprun published *L'Écriture ou la vie* in which he described his liberation from the Nazi concentration camp at Buchenwald, forty-nine years previously. Like so many other survivors of the Holocaust, Semprun spent the rest of his life trying to come to terms, not just with his experiences as a prisoner, but with the fact that he survived. This text stands as his testimony to the trauma of the camp, and to the arduous half-century he spent trying to find a way to write about it.

There is one particularly significant memory in this text that Semprun takes his time recounting. It is May 1945, Buchenwald has been liberated by the Americans, and Semprun finds himself in a hotel in Eisenach that is being used as a centre for repatriation. Spending a sleepless night with other ex-prisoners waiting for their transportation back home, he falls into a discussion. How, they wonder, will they ever manage to explain what has happened to them once they are in their own lands? To 'tell it like it was' is not so simple. How to describe experiences that are horrific beyond belief and unimaginable to the average person? The mountains of dead bodies, the monstrous incinerators, the mindless battle for survival, the bleak absence of hope. How to describe it in such a way that the listener does not flee in terror, or stare in blank incomprehension? And what is it about the camp experience that most needs to be understood? What is it most necessary to explain?

The young Semprun himself thinks he has the answer: 'On n'y parviendra pas sans un peu d'artifice. Suffisament d'artifice pour que ça devienne de l'art!' (You'll never manage it without a degree of artifice. Just enough artifice for it to become art!). Initially his companions disagree. What has art to do with the experiences they have just lived through? The idea of using fiction to portray the camps seems to betray the intense reality of their suffering. But Semprun has an eloquent ally who takes his side, a man he recognises as a French academic. This man points out that there will be many witness accounts of life in the camps, and eventually documentation will be uncovered that will also stand as evidence of the atrocities that have been committed. But a historical reconstruction of the concentration camps will not in itself bring alive the harrowing truth of the Holocaust: 'la vérité essentielle de l'expérience, n'est pas transmissible ... Ou plutôt, elle ne l'est que par l'écriture littéraire' (the essential truth of experience cannot be communicated ... Or rather, it can only be communicated through literary writing).

From 1945, when he has just lived through one of the worst experiences of the twentieth century, to 1994 in the heart of the media age, Semprun believed that only literature held the key to articulating the truth of his experience. Telling stories may seem old-fashioned, particularly nowadays in an era dominated by diverse visual media, but there is something unique about stories and their ability to provoke multiple, far-reaching effects. It would take Semprun a while to find the literary voice that would do justice to his account. As its title suggests, *L'Écriture ou la vie* is partially the story of his struggle to tell the 'essential truth' of the camps, and in a way that would not destroy his fragile and hard-won equilibrium as a survivor. But what Semprun comes to realise, and what would constitute one of the great artistic revelations of the twentieth century, is that the division between writing and life is just an illusion. Writing and living may seem like separate occupations, but they are wholly and fundamentally enmeshed in one another.

To make sense of life, we have to write about it. We have to tell stories, in the sense that we organise experience and then give it a meaning. And what modern narrative would come increasingly to realise was that the way we write about experience determines the sense we make of it. Semprun's text, like so many others in the century, is experimental. Its structure and format are unusual; it is fragmentary and digressive and does not have a final conclusion. While he does describe the traumatic conditions in the camps, much of the text passes in memories of books he has read that had a profound impact on him. Semprun's voice is not one long, dark tale of suffering and degradation. Instead he changes his perspective, understanding the feeling of imprisonment better through the eyes of the young Semprun who was so recently liberated, unable to explore what he calls the horror of evil except through the poetry and philosophy that he loved with passion. Semprun's story requires a unique format because his experience is so beyond the normal frames of reference. He can only make sense of his experience by comparing it to the everyday face of the world, by measuring the distance he has moved away from the realms of nightmare.

The Holocaust and its literature constitute only a tiny part of the vast twentieth century, but I mention it here because the extremity of the writing situation highlights very clearly some of the fundamental motivations in modern literary creation. There is a belief that is growing more prevalent in schools that literature is somehow irrelevant to the modern world, and that it can at best be used to illustrate social or historical conflicts. There could not be a greater misunderstanding of the point of literature. Semprun's text brings together some of the dominant themes of modern French literature in his quest to represent authentically the truth of an experience that defies expression. It is autobiographical, dealing with a limit experience (that is to say an experience at the very limit of what we can represent and understand), and as such it shows a man struggling to find words to express his experience. Semprun continually questions how he might achieve this, not out of some quaint academic interest in narrative, but because it really matters. There is an ethical imperative for everyone to know what happened in concentration camps so that such atrocities can never happen again. But it also matters personally for Semprun. Putting words to his experience, explaining how it happened, and what effect it had on him, he is rebuilding his identity with every sentence he writes. At a basic level, when something goes wrong our first response is usually to talk about it, and the way we recount the event firms up our initially confused feelings. For a concentration camp survivor, this simple mechanism is pushed to an extreme. Expressing 'la vérité essentielle' of the experience can mean the difference between sanity and insanity, life and suicide. Extreme experience brings with it the recognition that we are creatures of language, that language constitutes our very being, and self-expression provides our means of mental survival.

Exploring the link between identity and narrative is essential to understanding modern French literature, where we repeatedly find intimate, first-person narratives, concerned with detailing life through one particular, quirky, perspective. Often, as is the case with Semprun, these narratives represent individuals thrown into extreme situations, and the modern fascination with excess means that these texts explore murder and anarchy, rather than simple violence, eroticism rather than love, and madness rather than confusion. Yet it is often the case as well, that these events occur in the life of a protagonist who would otherwise be deemed 'ordinary', for modern texts seek to acknowledge how extraordinary, chaotic and unpredictable life has become. Modern literature pits its protagonists against the harshest historical circumstances, or against extremes of emotion. Texts focus on moments of great suffering, bewilderment, or dangerous fantasy, in order to explore the human psyche when it breaks down and fails. This is not as sadistic as it sounds. When cars break down we are forced to confront what lies under the bonnet, and human identity is just the same; its failure forces us to consider its very process of construction. Through examining individuals in crisis, literature takes a magnifying glass to the experience of existence. The twentieth century was obsessed with the question of what it is to be. How we perceive, what we desire, how we respond to the objects and people who surround us provided one of the distinct preoccupations of the century, and in modern French literature, from Proust to the Existentialists to contemporary interest in autobiography, writers have sought to dissect experience and to uncover the farthest reaches of human consciousness.

The obsession with explaining how we survive the trials of existence reflects a growing fear that such survival may be in doubt. Throughout the twentieth century the speed of social and political change and the violence of historical events have conspired to render individuals increasingly vulnerable to experience. Literature suggests that, paradoxically, the more information the century has supplied us with – in terms of our bodies, our awareness of world events, our understanding of the environment we inhabit –, the more fearful and vulnerable we have become. Although developments in medicine, physics and engineering have opened up vast new areas of knowledge, it is still not the kind of knowledge that could protect us from fear and alienation in the modern world. Modern French literature thus seeks a complementary relation to the other sciences, which may tackle the question of what it is to be human, but never the question of what it means. The link between identity and narrative, emphasised in these texts through their exploration of extreme experience, demonstrates how one essential area of what it means to be human (and one ideally suited to the work of literature) is our relationship to language, to its possibilities, challenges and frustrations. While it has always been the case that literature seeks to express liminal states, to defamiliarise the quotidian, and to find new voices for new realities, the excessive and demanding twentieth century has explored the nature and structure of language as never before.

The results have been diverse, with experimental texts that are at once playful and eccentric yet also anxious lest the limitations of language become unsurmountable. Semprun himself, with more reason than most to seek vital new forms of self-expression, defines the job of writing as: 'L'écriture, si elle prétend être davantage qu'un jeu, ou un enjeu, n'est qu'un long, interminable travail d'ascèse, une façon de se déprendre de soi en prenant sur soi' (Writing, if it claims to be more than a game, or a game with high stakes, is nothing more than a long, endless process of self-denial, a way of being liberated from one's self while calling it to account). This is a complicated concept, and it requires sustained thought to prise out Semprun's meaning, but he intends to slow down our reading and alert us to the subtleties of the language, which have a role to play in the message. Essentially, Semprun marries two thoughts here; the first that writing is a serious game, something that appears playful but is actually risky, and fraught with danger. The second is that what is put on the line, or rather what is put into the lines, is the self. The two unusual forms of the normally ordinary verb 'prendre' used here – 'déprendre de' meaning to lose one's fondness for something, and 'prendre sur' meaning to give up time or money – show how Semprun is making language work very hard to exceed its given boundaries and express a subtle idea. It is, as he suggests, hard labour to appraise oneself without sentimentality and then invest that self in the written word. But if writing can achieve this, then it ceases to be a simple experiment and becomes, instead, a result. If the intricate manipulation of language has such far-reaching consequences, it is no surprise that modern texts expend so much effort in exploring and experimenting with the words that make up their substance.

So, what modern French texts especially highlight is the very *act* of putting words to experience. As it has sought to push back the boundaries of expression, literature has become increasingly caught up in exploring its own creative practices, and in many texts other than the Semprun we find authors considering the process of writing as they engage with it. This self-reflexivity, as it is often termed, seeks to acknowledge the power language has not simply to represent what we experience, but to determine the experience itself. Our relationship not just to our selves, but also to the world around us, is by no means innocent and immediate; rather it is mediated through language. For the French, who have a natural taste for abstract theorising over the intricacies of language, and a fiercely held belief that language organises our personal and polit-ical situation, this recognition has quite naturally led to an understanding of literature as potentially revolutionary – that is to say, able to change the way we think and the way we live. By the 1950s and 1960s in France we see the *nouveaux romanciers* and the dramatists of the *théâtre de l'absurde* casting aside the innocence of their relation to language and dismantling the structures of their work in order to explore the insidious power of stories. For if we accept that we use stories to make sense of our lives, then we must also acknowledge that those stories are part of the foundations of our culture, the very justification for the value judgements we make and the rules by which we live. In this way, every member of a cul-ture has a vested interest, not just in telling their own story, but in listening carefully for what is hidden or elided in the stories of others.

France has a strong literary tradition of which it is immensely proud, through which it has continually criticised and challenged its dominant culture. The disciplines of literature, philosophy and the visual arts are deeply enmeshed in French life, and what we might consider quite abstract concerns with language and psychoanalysis are very much part of the way France appraises its national identity. Allied to this academic interest, and considered its natural counterpart, is a profound engagement with politics. As a nation the French have never heard of political apathy, and at heart their literature seeks to consider and analyse social situations as they affect the individual. In the twentieth century politics and literature had a particularly close, reciprocal relationship. A number of literary movements arose with the aim of linking art and politics more closely, for example the Surrealists in the 1920s and the Existentialists in the 1940s, and the student uprising of May 1968 was a literary revolution that demanded social change based on abstract, theoretical notions of how power was organised. Distinct and different as all these movements are, however, they have all been troubled by internal conflict and the fear that in the modern world collective action is far from certain of success.

If a dominant trend of modern life has been the failure of communities and collectives, it is difficult to know whether its consequence or its cause has been the sense that man is ever more isolated and alienated in society, abandoned to his fate in a time of instability and change. The modern Frenchman (and in the early half of the century it *is* a man) is as bound up in the march of history as his predecessors ever were, but history seems to have become such a sweeping, impersonal force that he is ever more disempowered within the circumstances that surround him. Modern French texts repeatedly anchor history to one individual's perspective, partly because history is better understood when we see its consequences on the individual, partly because it is the common experience to have history act upon us, rather than the other way round. But here the point of the intimate narrative perspective is not just to criticise history for its thoughtless treatment of individuals (although this is undeniably part of its aim), but also to tell stories that would otherwise be silenced. Writing by women, and from countries colonised by France, often tells well known stories from very different viewpoints. Those who are marginalised or oppressed are given a voice by literature, and it is easy to see, here, how telling a story is instantly a political act. Furthermore, writing by both women and postcolonial writers not only charts the battle with dominant culture, but also its often bewildering aftermath. Neither modern history, nor modern narrative, retains any faith in the notion of a conclusion that is a happy ever after.

In this way, as in so many others, literature is a critical, conflictual engagement with History. It challenges and questions and rebels. It undermines our casual assumptions and shatters our comforting conventions. It demands, not just that we care about its issues, but that we make the effort to understand the contradictions and paradoxes that lie at the heart of them. This can make reading literature difficult and demanding. But if literature across the ages is concerned with pushing back boundaries and opening up new perspectives on the world we live in, it is also concerned to seduce, entertain and affect its readers. On the very last page of *L'Écriture ou la vie*, Semprun recalls a moment when, crossing the camp alone late at night, he is overwhelmed by a sudden and senseless happiness, closely followed by the recognition that he would remember this moment for the rest of his life. It would be a heartless reader indeed who remained unmoved by this. So, literature may be challenging, but it is also immensely rewarding.

However experimental and abstract modern literature may be, it never stops seeking to express 'la vérité essentielle de l'expérience' so necessary to Semprun. In fact, experimentation in the modern age lies at the heart of creating texts that aspire to new levels of authenticity. Writing, as the texts I will discuss so ably demonstrate, is never an alternative to living, never an escapist or frivolous pursuit. Instead literary writing is a courageous and determined confrontation with the risky business of life in the twentieth century. My approach in this book is by no means a complete classification of the vast, diverse literature of the century. Instead I have explored precisely this interrelation of identity, narrative and history in its varying manifestations, either in influential literary movements, or as shaping factors across different genres: novels, poetry and plays. In all cases I have concentrated on texts where the writing is notably challenging and experimental. As a result these texts are not always comfortable to read, and they are often complex and resistant to easy mastery. The textual analyses I undertake in this book are simply intended to offer reading strategies to help students overcome their initial difficulties. They are by no means comprehensive or definitive. As will become apparent over the course of this book, one of the challenges made by modern French literature is to the very practice of reading itself. Modern texts in their complex ambiguity and their sophisticated playfulness demand wholehearted engagement, but refuse to satisfy the reader with easy answers or neat conclusions.

Reading in the twentieth century was understood as a practice with assumptions and expectations, and in order to startle readers out of their complacency those expectations were regularly undermined. If we are creatures of language then every day we are called upon to read far more than just works of literature. We read one another, we read the world around us, and we read the situations we find ourselves in. Modern French literature asks readers to examine and be aware of the processes of interpretation that we use as second nature. For in the processes of reading and interpreting, in the way that we use stories and story-telling techniques to organise and understand experience, we make of our lives a sprawling and dynamic work of art. A lengthy family saga interspersed with periods of comedy, tragedy and farce. The essential revelation of modern literature is that art is not separate from our lives; it is in fact the process by which we engage with and possess our lives, the means by which we raise our existence above the level of mindless, comatose being. Semprun came to realise that his equation 'writing or life' was a false one. There is only writing and life, in a mutually informative, but endlessly complex interaction.

Suggested reading

Jennifer Birkett and James Kearns, *A Guide to French Literature: From Early Modern to Postmodern* (Basingstoke: Macmillan, 1997). This excellent, comprehensive guide offers readings of a huge range of texts and has a particularly strong section on the twentieth century.

Christopher Robinson, *French Literature in the Twentieth Century* (New Jersey: Barnes & Noble; Newton Abbot: David & Charles, 1980). Organised by major themes, this guide to the twentieth century takes an intelligent, sophisticated approach.

Germaine Brée, *Twentieth-Century French Literature*, trans. Louise Guiney (Chicago & London: University of Chicago Press, 1983). This overview only goes as far as the 1970s but again its thematic organisation is helpful and it has a useful, if dated, glossary of authors.

Terry Eagleton, *Literary Theory: An Introduction* (Oxford & New York: Basil Blackwell, 1983). Critical theory is often an enlightening counterpart to the study of modern literature, and this introductory guide remains one of the very best.

1

First-Person Narratives:

The Voice of No Authority

Every story requires a narrator. Sometimes that narrator is invisible and the reader is presented with a seemingly impersonal account. But sometimes the narrator takes the centre stage, and the question of what he or she is like becomes essential to the story. For instance, I am the narrator of this book, but up until now I've been invisible, hiding behind the text, as you would in any case expect me to do. If, however, I start telling you about myself, about my life and my thoughts and feelings as I'm writing, then suddenly our relationship changes. If I kept it up, this would become a very different kind of book. The fact that a slight change in tone totally alters the reading experience shows how powerfully affecting the narrator's voice can be. When the protagonist of a story provides the narrative voice and addresses the reader directly, he or she slips insidiously into our consciousness, offering us that disquieting but fascinating view of existence through the eyes of another. Such first-person narrators offer compelling but often flawed testimonies. We recognise the partial, emotionally coloured, disingenuous nature of their narratives; the way we are not just being told a tale, but sold it, won over to its version of the truth. Using a first-person narrator can make a story come alive, but it also silences all the other possible viewpoints on the events it describes. The voice of the narrator is convincing simply because it is the only one we hear, and its aim will often be to distract the reader from the fact that it demands our understanding or compassion. However, in the twentieth century the experimental, poignant or provocative nature of the stories narrators had to tell would stretch the reader's understanding to breaking point.

The first-person narrator is an extremely popular device in modern literature, and it appears in a wide range of different narratives. One common factor in almost all these first-person accounts is the focus on highly unusual and often alarming situations in which narrators are pushed to the limit. Some narratives, like those born of the concentration camps, offered traumatic accounts of atrocities that sickened or appalled their readers. In the texts of the Surrealist movement, narrators buoyed up on drugs or drink made readers accompany them through their landscapes of dream and fantasy. In the philosophical and political texts of the Existentialists, narrators explored their feelings of malaise, both physical and metaphysical, in a world increasingly experienced as irrational and unstable. In all these cases, first-person narratives are used because they provide supposedly immediate accounts of events that would otherwise appear improbable or unbelievable. But the unusual situations of the narrator force us to reconsider the so-called 'truths' of existence which we take for granted. The persuasive strategies of the narrator are put to work to convince readers of the need to question traditional ways of thinking, perceiving and experiencing. The simplest way to do this is to take us through the narrator's own emotional odyssey, forcing the reader to experience what the narrator experiences, literally to see it through the narrator's eyes. Even the most quirky or perverse mental landscape can become convincing when the reader inhabits it from within.

So one of the main reasons why the first-person narrator is significant as a device is because it charts the interaction of the subject with the world it inhabits. This dual perspective – outwards to the experience of modern society and inwards to its effect on subjectivity – provides one reason for the importance of first-person narratives in twentieth-century literature. They alone spoke with authenticity of the alienation, confusion and angst that had become the destiny of each individual in a rapidly-changing, often brutal, oddly anonymous modern society. While these texts have a strong ethical streak, they often display a more playful and experimental side. If the modern world was becoming increasingly problematic to represent, so was the modern subject that inhabited it. Narrators were no longer the heroes of texts, instead they were more frequently marginal, vulnerable, troubled individuals, struggling to find the words that would represent their fragmented selves. As narrators spoke, so it became clear that their selves were nothing more than the stories they were telling. Increasingly in these texts the self was seen less as a stable entity with a distinct essence, and more and more the dynamic, fluid product of language. What this means is that no one was better placed than the narrator of a story to recognise the extent to which he or she was constituted by *nothing more* than the words of the narrative. What modern texts aimed to do was to show the reader that this was a general truth of the human condition, and not just the lot of the story-book narrator.

Reclaiming the past: Proust and the self as a work of art

The beginning of the century saw the publication of one of the greatest first-person narratives of all time. Marcel Proust's *À la recherche du temps perdu* (In Search of Lost Time, published 1913-1927), combined philosophical enquiry into the modern condition, the story of a young man's apprenticeship in art, and an analytic and stylistic exploration of what literature could and should be. In it the narrator recounts in fragmentary fashion the story of his life from childhood to middle-age. Despite the length of Proust's work (seven volumes), this is not a complete and comprehensive account. Instead it is marked by partiality and a lyrical meandering style. There are few plotlines that progress, conflicts remain unresolved, and there are no dramas, crises or violent deaths. Instead the narrator concentrates on the trivial and the everyday; the routines of his childhood, his life in society, his failed love affairs, his increasingly sophisticated appreciation of art.

Art saturates the novel; not only the consideration of other artists, not just the process involved in appreciating art, but at the heart of the work, an enquiry into the way a work of art evolves. *À la recherche du temps perdu* concerns itself with art in general, but only in order to focus on its own process of production. Marcel's story is that of his lifetime's achievement – an apprenticeship in art that teaches him, like an ancient alchemist, to transform the base material of life into the burnished gold of literature. But the story is that of his gradual awakening and revelation, so that only in the final volume does he understand that ideal art restores 'notre vraie vie, la réalité telle que nous l'avons sentie et qui diffère tellement de ce que nous croyons' (our authentic existence; reality as we experienced it, which differs so much from what we believe it to be), and that: 'le seul livre vrai, un grand écrivain n'a pas, dans le sens courant, à l'inventer, puisqu'il existe déjà en chacun de nous, mais à le traduire' (to write the only truthful book, a great writer does not need to invent, in the common understanding of the term, but to translate, since it exists already inside each of us).

Theorising this act of translation – brute reality into ideal work of art – provides a major theme of the novel, but of course it is happening from the very first page we read. Marcel does not begin as a bad narrator and transform into an accomplished one. Instead the text mobilises two different chronologies; the time of writing through the voice of the older, wiser Marcel, and the perspective of the past through the young Marcel who experiences, suffers and fails. At each moment in the text, the events experienced by young Marcel are filtered through the rich, sedimentary layers of time, forming associations with other events, provoking analysis or speculation, and ultimately revelation as meaning or significance is uncovered. The voice that speaks to us offers what Edmund White describes as 'the transcript of a mind thinking' (138). The reader is cocooned in an intensely inner world of memory and dream, lost in Proust's lush, labyrinthine sentences, caught up in the very processes of perception and analysis. Unique in its time, Proust's work featured a narrator who considered the act of writing as it occurred; this self-reflexivity would come to dominate the art of the century.

If Proust highlighted the act of artistic creativity, he also explored what was at stake in the act of reading. Marcel remembers Sunday afternoons spent reading in the garden of his grandmother's house at Combray, describing the magic transformation wrought by a book: 'il déchaîne en nous pendant une heure tous les bonheurs et tous les malheurs possibles dont nous mettrions dans la vie des années à connaître quelques-uns, et dont les plus intenses ne nous seraient jamais révélés parce que la lenteur avec laquelle ils se produisent nous en ôte la perception' (For the space of an hour it unleashes within us all the possible joys and misfortunes of life. It would take us years to know but a few, and the most intense would never be revealed to us for their development is so slow as to render them almost imperceptible). This fits in with Marcel's understanding of literature as an ideal distillation of experience, a totality and a plenitude of experience that life denies us but which art restores. Reading gives us back experience that we didn't understand or appreciate at the time.

But reading is essential to the art of living as well. Large tracts of the narrative pass in stories of love and society, partly because this is the sum of Marcel's life, the time wasted and lost in frivolous pursuits that he seeks to regain, partly also because the domains of the lover and *le monde* (society) both seem oddly full of meaning which, over time, he recognises has to be read. Lovers and *les mondaines* (socialites) both offer systems of behaviour that are initially mysterious and require decipherment. High society has fixed requirements for those wishing to join the elite, and fixed sets of rules for behaviour and discourse within its limits that must not be transgressed. Such coded systems of meaning are at once obvious and relatively easy to learn. More troublesome and sophisticated are the sign systems of loved ones. Lovers, like social acquaintances, are at once wholly familiar and completely unknowable. But unlike those we meet in society, lovers matter too much to us: 'Les êtres nous sont d'habitude si indifférents que, quand nous avons mis dans l'un d'eux de telles possibilités de souffrance et de joie pour nous, il nous semble appartenir à un autre univers' (Other people are generally a matter of such indifference to us that when we invest in someone such possibilities for joy and for suffering they seem to belong to a different universe). Love provokes a reaction that is disproportionate, illogical or just plain eccentric, and thus demands to be analysed.

One of the best known sections of *À la recherche* is *Un amour de Swann* (Swann in love), in which Marcel recounts the disastrous love affair between the friend of his family, M. Swann, and Odette de Crécy, a woman of lower social standing and dubious morals. They are mismatched in terms of class and initially only mildly attracted to one another, and Swann's passion for Odette is only aroused when, one evening, he fails to find her where he expects her to be. Instantly his jealousy is awakened, and once he has started to suffer for Odette he begins truly to desire her. Jealousy is an important motivator in all the love affairs in *A la recherche*. Jealousy focuses the mind, and Swann is determined to know the 'truth' of Odette's behaviour, no matter how painful it might be for him. His thoughts are entirely occupied by her, he is overwhelmed with desire for her, and in this intoxicating, if desperate, state he is finally experiencing the kind of self-revelations that only love can provide. Proust is cynical about love; it is usually a humiliating and shaming experience, causing more pain than ecstasy. Love is rarely reciprocated by the beloved and the lover is left to project his own fantasies and longings onto her enigmatic form. Yet if the other person remains forever unknowable, love is not without its benefits; the intensity of its experience illuminates the psyche of the one who loves, offering a rich and revealing form of self-perception. Being in love is what counts, to the extent that the people we love are irrelevant. Being in love sets us off on a trajectory for knowledge and meaning, and this search Proust considers to be the basis for art.

We can properly talk of society and lovers as consisting of sign systems, because the messages they send out contain meaning in excess of what is immediately apparent. Gestures, words, simple acts seem significant in a way that exceeds their basic nature. To this category we can add what Naomi Segal terms 'banal objects', of which the most famous must be the madeleine cake. When the narrator eats a spoonful of madeleine dipped in tea, he is transported back to Combray and his aunt Léonie's house where he spent the holidays as a boy. A tidal wave of joyful emotions sweeps through him: 'Il m'avait aussitôt rendu les vicissitudes de la vie indifférentes, ses désastres inoffensifs, sa brièveté illusoire, de la même façon qu'opère l'amour, en me remplissant d'une essence précieuse: ou plutôt cette essence n'était pas en moi, elle était moi. J'avais cessé de me sentir médiocre, contingent, mortel' (Immediately I was rendered indifferent to the vicissitudes of life; its disasters seemed tame, its brevity an illusion. As if I were in love, I was filled with a precious essence, or rather, this essence was not within me, but part of me. I had ceased to feel mediocre, contingent, and mortal). The strength of Marcel's response to such an innocent action indicates that it is not necessarily the madeleine itself which contains the secret of his reaction. What matters is the world of Combray which the madeleine returns to him by reactivating forgotten senses.

Although it will take Marcel another six volumes to work out the full import of his discovery, he is experiencing a moment of involuntary memory, the return of the past in a perfect, complete and timeless form. As opposed to voluntary memory – the sterile mechanics of conscious intelligence – involuntary memory is the miraculous rediscovery of 'un peu de temps à l'état pur' (a moment of time in its purest form). What is meant by this is a kind of unhoped-for plenitude in the act of recollection. It is a chance to live a moment again, in the richness and unexpected immediacy of perfect sensory recall; sights, scents, sounds, textures, colours, emotions all return to Marcel, and return to him perfected, idealised and isolated from the distracting flow of existence There are only a handful of such occurrences across the length of *À la recherche*, and their nature as 'fortuite, inévitable' (fortuitous, inevitable) only serves to make them more precious to Marcel.

Spectacular as involuntary memory may be, why does it have the power for Marcel 'à me rendre la mort indifférente' (to make death a matter of indifference to me)? When so much is given to us in this work, where every sentence is saturated with philosophical thoughts and strong emotions, it is easy to forget that it is a novel about the pain and frustration of loss. Time performs its terrible process of attrition, wearing down our childhood selves, dispersing friends and lovers, taking us away from the places we knew. The narrative is entirely retrospective, looking back across the landscape of a life that is near its completion; it is a narrative of memories, and its non-linear structure attests to the fragmentary nature of memory itself. Proust's rich, abundant style weaves abstract thought and chains of association into the fissures and gaps, distracting us from what is missing. We never know, for instance, how Swann comes to marry Odette, when in the final sentence of his tale he has fallen out of love with her. Involuntary memory, by contrast, proves that there is some kind of coherent identity that exists despite the ravages of time. The past is not lost forever, but is simply buried in a time capsule that chance circumstances can split open, releasing the perfectly preserved contents within. Marcel suffers from his fallibility, his weak, contingent mortality, but involuntary memory shows that Marcel himself is the container of the essence of the past. The madeleine provokes the recall, but the memories of Combray are retained from his own internalised experience.

So, involuntary memory returns the past in an idealised form. Knowing as we do that Marcel believes only art has the power to idealise and perfect, we can see how he believes that memory is artistic, and the Marcel who is subject to involuntary memory is naturally an artist. However, this lengthy work charts his realisation that perfect recreation is not enough to make art. Instead description must be saturated with feeling, just as physical sensations must be understood with the help of abstract thought. It is this linking together of apparently disparate domains of experience – vivid sensory evocation and cool metaphysics, the rambling associative world of dream and fantasy with piercing intellectual observations – that makes Proust's style so innovative, and so metaphorical. Bringing together past and present or mind and body, by finding the linking factors between them, provides the underlying structure of Proust's thought and his art. Marcel's distinctive narrative voice is a mixture of poetic enchantment and detached microscopic self-examination. It aims to reproduce not a realistic portrayal of a world, but a representation of the experience of living a particular, inner reality. Marcel's explorations in the creation of art produce a detailed exploration of the way that we perceive, and the possibilities we have for representing those perceptions. In other words, for the first time, finding a way to express subjectivity becomes a story in itself.

Proust's work provided a compendium of experimental possibilities for the rest of the century to explore and develop. One of the most significant legacies of *À la recherche* would be the confusion between life and art, between autobiography and fiction. Proust's narrator is also called Marcel, and his struggle to recapture lost experience is written with such authenticity it is hard to believe it is not autobiographical. But although Proust's own life did feed into his work in disguised and complicated ways, the final result is fiction. Where the confusion between life and art becomes significant is in the process of transformation that Proust highlights, between lived experience and the written word on the page. How to represent experience with accuracy and precision would become a dominant concern of the century. It is equally prevalent in the work of another of the most influential writers of the early twentieth century, André Gide, whose minimalist style provides an interesting counterpoint to the exotic excesses of Proust.

Rewriting the past: the mask of sincerity

André Gide was a contemporary of Proust who was successful when Proust was still unknown. In fact, as head of the publishers,

Gallimard, Gide was responsible for turning down Proust's first volume, put off by Proust's reputation as a socialite and a snob, thus obliging him to pay for its publication. Gide lived to regret this when the book won the Prix Goncourt. He was a highly respected author in his own right enjoying a distinguished and varied literary career, publishing *récits*, a novel, plays, journals and travel writing. His own series of first-person narratives, in this instance confessional *récits*, provide a fascinating contrast to Proust's work. Both authors confused autobiography and fiction but in very different ways. Gide considered that his texts provided a kind of controlled space for experimentation in which he explored extreme versions of his own dilemmas. In Gide's texts the unresolvable conflict lies between the desire for a mystical union with God, which finds its basis in self-denial and constraint, and an insatiable hunger for life and its pleasures, which incites the individual to explore his potential to the full.

Gide was brought up in a strictly Protestant family, but experienced a kind of hedonistic awakening on a trip to Africa at the age of 24. From this time on he struggled to reconcile the opposing forces of his nature. Two of his *récits*, *L'Immoraliste* (The Immoralist, 1902) and *La Porte étroite* (Straight is the Gate, 1909), usually read as companion texts, explore these contradictory desires. In *L'Immoraliste*, Michel recovers from a serious attack of tuberculosis, determined to live life to the full. But the zeal and aggression with which he attempts to master his life have a large impact on others, and his authentic longing for freedom becomes difficult to distinguish from a selfish, egotistic quest for pleasure. By contrast, in *La Porte étroite*, Alissa's desire to embody virtue leads her away from a relationship with the narrator, Jérôme. Although she genuinely loves him, the desire for an intense form of spiritual purity makes her scorn an easy domestic contentment, and Jérôme's weakness and apathy mean that he offers little resistance. In both cases the protagonists pursue their ideals to excess, unable or unwilling to compromise. In both cases, their single-mindedness results in tragedy.

A third *récit* of Gide's is equally well known. In *La Symphonie pastorale* (Pastoral Symphony, 1919), the pastor saves a young orphan, Gertrude, from poverty and deprivation, bringing her up in his own home and educating her with a highly selective brand of Christian teaching. Gertrude is blind, but the real blindness at stake is the pastor's wilful ignorance of his desire for the girl and the distress this causes his own family. While this seems straightforwardly immoral, Gide's talent lies in making simplistic ethical judgements impossible. Although we condemn the pastor, Michel and Alissa for their lack of self-awareness, the first-person narrative style offers an intimate and vivid picture of their complex humanity. We are presented with engaging and sophisticated portraits of individuals who would be saints, even if to do so they end up as hopeless sinners.

The narrators in these texts, then, have something specific to say, a particular story to tell, and a particular reason for telling it. The implicit motivation for narrating is one of self-justification, and what this tends to highlight is the hidden, secretive elements of the story. In each case the narrator stresses the honesty and integrity with which he will recount his tale. Michel asks himself: 'que n'importe à moi ce récit, s'il cesse d'être véritable?' (what use is this account to me if it ceases to be truthful?). But this is also an aside to his audience in case the rhetorical question turns out to be a proper enquiry after all. Because we hear no voice except that of the narrator, whom we know to have an agenda, the reader is left searching the subtext for the truth of what happened. There is no voice outside the story that could offer useful commentary, and so the onus of interpretation falls upon the reader. This interpretation is difficult to excavate from a text that concentrates on recounting events at the expense of emotional shading. It wastes no words (quite the opposite of Proust who never uses one word where twenty would do), and presents a stylistically minimal account of psychologically complicated relationships. Gide's texts are deceptively simple, and in that simplicity lies the deception. The smooth easy-reading surface of the text belies the profound undercurrents of troubled emotion. The narrator's 'straightforward' tales are masterpieces of ambiguity and omission, yet at the same time, Gide asks searching questions about the very possibility of sincerity. Often enquiries into Gide's works are structured around the opposition between sincerity and hypocrisy, or what Gide called the *être* (being) and the *paraître* (appearance). The *paraître* or the outward appearance of the individual is often nothing more than a mask of social conventions and moral clichés that hides the more genuine, less appealing motivations of the *être*. Yet the confessional récit suggests that the psychological situation is more complex still. If we consider *L'Immoraliste* in some detail briefly, we can explore the tensions inherent in Michel's moral position. Michel's return to health is more than a convalescence, it is 'une augmentation, une recrudesence de vie' (an upsurge, a fresh outburst of life), which reveals to him, not a way of life that he thinks he would like to live, but a more genuine selfhood which he believes he has denied: 'l'être authentique [...] celui que tout, autour de moi, livres, maîtres, parents, et que moi-même avions tâché d'abord de supprimer' (the authentic being [...] the person whom everything around me, books, teachers, parents, even myself, had at first conspired to suppress). So Michel's position is set out in spuriously moral terms; he wants to be himself, which is to say he wants to submit to his overwhelming lust for life, for freedom, and for what appears to be transgressive forms of pleasure.

The behaviour that Michel privileges is not described to the reader, but rather shown to us in episodes free from comment. For instance, while he convalesces, Marceline brings local children in to distract him. He dislikes those that Marceline prefers, finding them 'faibles, chétifs, et trop sages' (weak, sickly and too well-behaved), reminiscent, then, of his old self. Only one in particular stands out; this is Moktir who appeals to him by stealing a small pair of scissors. Michel is watching him in a mirror when this happens, meaning that Moktir does not know he is observed. The power-play at work here is complicated and intriguing: Moktir is the one stealing, but Michel is watching with pleasure, not just allowing, but silently encouraging him to steal. This would seem to put him in control of the situation. Yet he is also the victim of the crime, watching himself be robbed. 'À partir de ce jour Moktir devint mon préféré' (from that day onwards, Moktir became my favourite), he tells us baldly and enigmatically. A similar situation occurs when Michel and Marceline return to France to La Morinière, a farm Michel has inherited. Michel takes to going poaching at night with the disreputable Alcide. Once again he is the willing voyeur of crime that occurs on his own property. It would seem that Michel is fascinated by bad behaviour, but he is never the instigator of crime, only its witness, and indeed the fact that he gives up his own possessions shows how he keeps that trangressive force contained within his own domains. The 'selfish hedonism' which troubles the serenity of his new-found desires, is actually a rather timid and passive trait, inward-looking and far from violent.

Where Michel's behaviour does appear to invite question is in his treatment of Marceline, the wife he takes to appease his dying father. Marceline nurses him through his illness, and for this act of devotion she is quietly and covertly despised. Although Michel repeats relentless declarations of love for Marceline, she can do no right. When he is ill 'j'étais gêné par sa présence'(her presence made me uncomfortable). When he is cured her love for him seems both excessive and insufficient, and he complains: 'elle m'aimait trop déjà pour me bien voir' (she loved me too much to see me clearly). The implication is that the person Marceline loves is his old, discarded self which he no longer values. He consistently attributes to Marceline a preference for all that is vulnerable, weak or virtuous, although where Marceline's true desires may lie is a mystery. We see her only through Michel's eyes and his self-serving perceptions. Yet by forcing his perceptions on her she eventually becomes the weak person he thinks she is. The turning point in the *récit* comes when Michel averts a potentially fatal carriage accident, finally consummates his marriage and feels at last in his rightful position of superiority over Marceline. Afterwards he wonders: 'Devrai-je un jour, à mon tour, te soigner? M'inquiéter pour toi, Marceline?'(Will I have to care for you in my turn, one day? Will I have to worry about you, Marceline?). Curiously enough his renewed health and vigour seem to come at the cost of his wife's wellbeing. From now on their positions reverse as Marceline becomes sickly. But look after her is precisely what Michel does not do: instead he neglects her. She miscarries his child, falls ill, and dies.

It is here, in the black heart of the power struggle between Michel and his wife, that the 'confession' falls most silent, and yet speaks most eloquently. Michel's errors are etched on the body of Marceline. She is his innocent victim, yet at first sight it is difficult to know why her death should seem so inevitable. In all three of Gide's *récits* a similar structure can be traced; a male narrator who speaks, and a woman, ostensibly the object of affection, who dies. Both

Alissa and Gertrude pay with their lives for stubborn, self-centred, self-justificatory narrators. Although they are not allowed voices in the narrative (with the exception of Alissa's edited diary), they reflect the truth of the men's actions, rather than the carefully wrought truth of their confessions. From the earliest stages of *L'Immoraliste* we can see how Marceline is made into Michel's scapegoat. In Michel's reading of their relationship they are continually placed in opposition, Marceline increasingly coming to represent and embody all the weakness and falliblity that Michel detests. But this is Michel's projection onto Marceline; her reality is denied in order that he can feel secure in his new incarnation as strong and active. His need to make Marceline his inferior is telling, however. His hatred of weakness is excessive and indicates his fear of it, a fear that reveals how close he still is to that part of his self. Despite his protestations of newly-discovered heroism, Michel is still fighting a feminised part of himself. Even in her illness Marceline saves him by allowing him to define himself as the strong partner, yet his apathy and purposelessness once she dies reveals this to be yet another hollow protestation.

Whereas in Proust, what mattered was what the self could absorb and retain from the outside world, in Gide, the self is always created in contradistinction to what surrounds it. To be strong Michel must eradicate all traces of weakness from himself, and Marceline must bear them for him. The 'shocking' confession he makes of his desire to be among lowly criminals is an illusory vice that fails to prove he is strong, or that he is fulfilling repressed potential. Marceline's insight into this is literally fatal, for it reveals a truth he cannot bear to acknowledge. She says 'Ne comprenez-vous pas que notre regard développe, exagère en chacun le point sur lequel il s'attache? Et que nous faisons devenir ce que nous prétendons qu'il est?' (Don't you understand that we develop and exaggerate the image we have of a person that pleases us most? And that we make them into what we believe them to be?). This is a perceptive judgement, particularly when turned back onto Michel himself. Marceline recognises his authentic heroic persona for the comforting charade that it is, and shortly after this she dies.

Gide's narratives showcase complex, fallible narrators attempting to hide their neuroses through a display of narrative willpower. As the century progressed, the need to conceal weakness was dispensed with, and a new generation of anti-heroes arrived.

What actually happened in the past? Beckett and the art of confusion

Some of the most alarming and astonishing anti-heroes can be found in the works of Samuel Beckett, an Irishman who followed the European avant-garde to Paris and began writing in French. Arguably best known for his play, *En Attendant Godot* (Waiting for Godot, 1948), Beckett also wrote a series of first-person narratives that are closest to monologues or stream-of-consciousness novels. Stream-of-consciousness, as its name suggests, is often less involved in telling a story than in describing the perceptions of the narrator at the moment that they occur. In Beckett's novels, plot is marginal to the narrative, although this is usually because the narrator is not sure exactly what, if anything, has happened. Beckett plunges the reader into the world of the narrator, a world of physical decrepitude, social alienation and radical mental confusion. Beckett's narrators are tramp-like figures with no homes or families, no jobs, no lives in the conventional sense. Instead their time is spent confronting the uncertainties of existence, although confrontation is too strong a word for their brand of reflexive bewilderment. Beckett's texts are problematic and challenging and relentlessly subversive about the things we take for granted, but they are also richly, blackly humorous. Often the humour of Beckett's narratives gets lost in discussion of their more serious aspects and yet it provides an immediate and viable response to the absurdities of existence that would otherwise be too bleak to contemplate.

All the narratives I have been discussing in this chapter are involved with the link between identity and narrative, or the understanding that the way we tell a story reveals something about our fears and desires. What is significant for both Proust and Gide is the belief that, no matter how difficult it may be to express oneself authentically, language is nevertheless transparent to meaning; it says what it means, and it can say something truthful about experience. For Beckett, the relationship between language and the subjects who use it has taken a distinct turn for the worse. In Beckett language may mean something (although this is sometimes in doubt), but what it means is on a different level altogether to the reality it purports to communicate.

Beckett's texts ask us difficult questions: what if language is a system that does not represent reality, but gives false order to the chaos that we experience? What if we can never say what we mean, exactly, and following on from this, how do we ever know what it is that we mean to say? Molloy, the narrator of the novel of the same name (published 1951), spends much narrative space pondering such issues: 'il m'arrivait souvent, du temps où je parlais encore, d'avoir trop dit en croyant avoir dit trop peu, et d'avoir trop peu dit en croyant avoir dit trop. Je veux dire qu'à la réflexion, à la longue plutôt, mes excès de paroles s'avéraient pauvretés et inversement' (it often happened to me, at the time when I was still speaking, to have said too much when I thought I had said too little, and to have said too little, thinking I had said too much. I mean that on reflection, or rather over time, my linguistic excesses turned out to be insufficiencies, and vice versa). Of course Molloy speaks at some length about this difficulty, not simply expressing but performing the act of speaking too much (or inadequately) while not saying anything much at all.

In his texts, Beckett makes us realise the extent to which language is tricky and elusive, containing more within its phrases than is necessary or helpful, and yet never managing to express anything with precision. Over the course of the narrative it seems to have a life of its own, running away with the narrator, who is loquacious but far from in control of his utterances. Sometimes, however, what can seem like absurdities on the part of the narrator hint at a more profound disturbance within narrative. The odd phrase in the above quotation 'du temps où je parlais encore' strikes the reader as peculiar, particularly when the intimate stream-of-consciousness sounds exactly as if the narrator were speaking within the reader's head. One reasonable literal interpretation is that Molloy can no longer speak, but can still write (this is entirely possible given Molloy's many and increasing physical disabilities). But other clues in the text work to problematise the concept of the narrator narrating. It is often impossible – not just in this text, but in any first-person narrative you care to think of – for the narrator to be writing at the time that he is experiencing. The immediacy of first-person narratives is therefore often an illusion, a trick of the narrative's structure, or part of a pact the reader makes to suspend disbelief. *Molloy* highlights the distance that exists between the narrator who supposedly speaks and perceives and the actual moment of the text's production, while maintaining a narrative voice that could not be more immediate or spontaneous.

The role of the narrator becomes increasingly troubled. Not only can he not say what he means, not only are we unsure that he can be the origin for the narrative, but the entire story he has to tell us is repeatedly put in doubt. When the narrative opens, Molloy is alone in a room that could be his mother's, which he may have inherited, if he were sure that his mother were dead: 'Était-elle déjà morte à mon arrivée? Ou n'est-elle pas morte que plus tard? Je veux dire morte à enterrer. Je ne sais pas. Peut-être ne l'a-t-on pas enterrée encore' (Was she already dead when I arrived? Or did she die later? I mean dead as in ready for burial. I don't know. Perhaps she hasn't been buried yet). Yet the entire quest which fuels the narrative (such as it is) is to return to his mother, to see her again. Where his mother is, and whether or not she is alive, is in some ways the least of his problems. The relationship between them is impossible to define: describing it, Molloy says: 'Moi, je la prenais pour ma mère et elle, elle me prenait pour mon père' (I took her for my mother, she took me for my father), and often he fantasises that women he meets or met in the past could have been his mother, even transposing the role onto past lovers (if they were indeed lovers). The most straightforward and obvious of relationships, that between mother and son, is subjected to all kinds of distortion, and the result of this, ultimately, is to make the boundaries of the self very unstable. We cannot know anything about Molloy because he does not know anything about himself.

This is not simply because narrative is unreliable, with its urge to make sense of what is disordered and irrational, but because the experience underlying the narrative is uncertain. Partly this is caused by the imperfections of memory, and partly because Molloy did not know exactly what happened at the very moment of its occurrence. With so many levels of uncertainty in place, any kind of coherent identity that Molloy makes for himself is necessarily fictional, that is to say, a product of the narrative he writes. Molloy's self is shapeless, unlimited, fragmentary; what happens to him is a matter of conjecture. His own response to experience, filtered as it is through the tricky medium of language, can never be satisfactorily expressed. Therefore to talk of Molloy as a 'character' is to use language to construct him over the top of his boundless, fluid and undefinable relationship to his existence. And this is more or less what the narrative does, for even if it is artificial and at one remove from the reality it describes, all use of language must reveal the existence of a speaking subject, even if it does so only by tracing the ghostly contours of where a conventional self might possibly be.

While the voice of Molloy is fascinating, if frustrating, the text *Molloy* is made up of two sections, of which the second is narrated by the alter ego of Molloy, named Moran. When this half of the narrative begins, Moran is everything Molloy is not; in control, definite, lucid, looking after a son and a house and holding down a job. However, this tale is one of 'disintegration and metamorphosis' to use Michael Sheringham's terms, in which Moran is sent by his mysterious bosses, Youdi and Gaber, to find Molloy. Already eccentricities creep into a seemingly conventional account: Moran tells us: 'Et la voix que j'écoute, je n'ai pas eu besoin de Gaber pour me le transmettre. Car elle est en moi et elle m'exhorte à être jusqu'au bout le fidèle serviteur que j'ai toujours été, d'une cause qui n'est pas la mienne [...] Et cela dans la haine de mon maître et le mépris de ses desseins'(And as for the voice I listen to, I didn't need Gaber to pass on its message. For it is inside me, exhorting me to be to the bitter end the faithful servant I have always been, to a cause that is not my own [...] And this while hating my master and despising his plans). Hearing these disembodied voices, Moran sets off into what soon becomes wilderness in search of Molloy. Inevitably, during this quest (the point of which he forgets along the way) he comes increasingly to resemble Molloy, in terms of his deteriorating physical state, and his perceptual uncertainties. Eventually his authority and aggression disintegrate until he is left with 'd'enfantins espoirs' (childish hopes) that his son (who disappeared en route) will return to him, or that Molloy himself will come and save him as 'un ami, un père' (a friend, a father). Eventually he finds his way home, but the journey has transformed him. The narrative ends in radical self-contradiction: 'Il est minuit. La pluie fouette les vitres. Il n'était pas minuit. Il ne pleuvait pas' (It is midnight. Rain whips the window panes. It was not midnight. It wasn't raining).

So what are we to make of this? This narrative appeals to that of Molloy through a series of ironic echoes. In fact reading it we are drawn away from the initially conventional narrative of Moran and back towards the nonsensical, problematic narrative of Molloy, as if this were somehow inevitable. Indeed, the control that Moran exerts over his household is highly tenuous, even while it is excessive and violent. It is only, then, by an extreme force of will that he manages to maintain an air of authority. Once he moves outside the domain of his house, both desert him. There is a suggestion here that will and authority are all that divide coherence from incoherence in narrative, and that narrative is more authentic, closer to reality as we experience it, when it casts aside its spurious logic and rationality and tunes in to the fluid and formless progression of existence. Molloy's narrative, then, would offer a more profound representation of existence, but one that generally we cover up in favour of the meaningful, conventional forms of narrative. The problems Molloy experiences with language and narrative are problems inherent in language and narrative, but pushed to an extreme.

What is interesting is that Moran should provide the only father figure in the narrative, and that his paternal qualities of authority and control should be the ones he loses most dramatically. By the middle of the twentieth century the notion of a father figure in charge of a narrative was simply no longer viable. Yet Moran's transformation is not an act of humiliation, rather it is a process of redemption. He becomes 'de plus en plus faible et content' (increasingly weak and happy) and has of his identity 'un sens plus net et vif qu'auparavant, malgré ses lésions intimes et les plaies dont elle se couvrait'(a more vivid and distinct sense than before, despite its internal injuries and the wounds with which it is covered). Dispensing with certainty, control, structure and authority was increasingly to be seen as reaching a new height of authenticity in narrative, while also providing fresh creative impetus and drive to modern literature. Art would be transformed by its urge to experiment, to find new ways of expressing the new, confusing modern world, and the plight of those who inhabited it. Identity, in all its complexity, would fascinate authors and playwrights who, in their urge to explore deep into the human mind, would often concentrate on the perplexing and sordid aspects of mankind. And of course, the unimaginable tragedy of two world wars would add a poignant ethical necessity to the exploration. Weakness, fallibility, and anxiety would increasingly provide the impetus for the protagonists of twentieth-century narrative, and the exploration of the darker side of humanity, in its devices and desires, would come to dominate modern literature.

Suggested reading

Edmund White, *Proust* (London: Weidenfeld & Nicolson, 1999). This is more of a biography than a critique, but it is so engaging and offers such perceptive insights it provides an excellent introduction to the life and the works.

Malcolm Bowie, *Proust, Jealousy, Knowledge* (London: University of London, 1978). Malcolm Bowie is one of the very best commentators on Proust. This is one of his early works but it remains a classic study.

Naomi Segal, *The Banal Object: Theme and Thematics in Proust, Rilke, Hofmannsthal, and Sartre* (London: Institute of Germanic Studies, University of London, 1981). This is not a book devoted to Proust but the section on his work provides an excellent point of entry into a reading of the entire text.

David H. Walker, *André Gide* (London: Macmillan, 1990). A comprehensive, lucid and continually engaging critique of his work.

Michael Lucey, *Gide's Bent: Sexuality, Politics, Writing* (Oxford: Oxford University Press, 1995). An individual but rewarding perspective on Gide's work, tackling once and for all that vexed issue of his homosexuality.

Michael Sheringham, *Beckett: Molloy* (London: Grant & Cutler, 1985). This series of student's guides to texts is often excellent and this comprehensive exploration of Molloy is both accessible and sophisticated.

Thomas Tresize, *Into the Breach: Samuel Beckett and the Ends of Literature* (Princeton: Princeton University Press, 1990). So much has been written on Beckett it is difficult to choose, but this recent text considering issues of subjectivity is both challenging and interesting.

2

Modern Poetry:

The Witchcraft of Words

Moving on to poetry from first-person narrative may seem an abrupt change of literary landscape, but really the two are not so very dissimilar in their concerns. Essentially poets are particularly sophisticated narrators, who are still interested in finding new forms of expression for their experiences, and who trust and value above all else their feelings, instincts, dreams and fears. Modern poetry is also similar to modern narrative in that the need to experiment motivates its creation. But from this point onwards, all similarity ends.

One of my favourite descriptions of the art of poetry is the phrase: 'superbly condensed verbal theatre'. It conveys the intensity and the drama of the poem, grand ideas struggling and clashing by means of an intricate choreography in which every word has a significant role to play. Readers of poetry are similar to theatregoers in that the best form of appreciation is to sit back and let the poem happen, emotions and attention engaged, of course, but acknowledging that poetry is a spectacle of words that demands nothing but awe and admiration. There is no place for the kind of tidy-minded intervention that desires loose ends to be tucked away and meaning to be conveyed in neatly tied bundles. This is one possible reason why poetry can be so confusing and difficult to read. We must respond to it as if it were a piece of explosive cinema, or on other occasions a particularly complex magician's trick, but to read it requires a slow and meticulous concentration on each word. By the time we have puzzled over the awkward vocabulary and unscrambled the confusing syntax, the effort required can seem far greater than the reward. Being an impatient reader myself I would far rather gobble up a novel than chew through a poem. But this is

2. *Modern Poetry*   37

where modern poetry has certain advantages. Unlike the lengthy screeds of nineteenth-century poetry, modern poems do tend to be short, concentrated bursts of verbal fireworks, difficult, magnificent and provocative. This makes them harder to treat as if they were a kind of tortuous prose, and so prevents the sort of reading that turns them into unsatisfactory novels. It helps to remember that poetry is a very particular literary genre, and modern French poetry a specific subset within that.

What, then, is poetry? At the start of the century, when literary criticism as a theory and a practice was founded, this was the very first question that was posed. It was acknowledged that poetry was the most supremely literary of all literary forms, and so it must, therefore, contain the key to understanding what distinguished the literary from other forms of writing. The most obvious way of identifying poetry is simply to see what it looks like on the page. Unlike prose which comes in blocks of type, poetry is divided into stanzas of fixed structure, and French poetry of previous centuries is rigidly regulated by metre. 'Metre' means that each line must contain a certain number of syllables. The famous 'alexandrine', or a line of twelve syllables, is often considered to be the classic unit of French poetry. In fact the alexandrine so dominated French verse that when Victor Hugo presumed in his 1830 play, *Hernani*, to split an alexandrine (separating the noun 'escalier' or 'staircase' at the end of one line from the adjective 'dérobé' or 'hidden' at the beginning of the next, thus breaking the rule that each alexandrine should contain complete units of syntax and meaning), the theatre spectators were in uproar; an indication, if nothing else, of the classy type of theatre-goer in nineteenth-century France. But from this point on experimentation with poetic structure became the fashion, and the work of Symbolist poets such as Rimbaud and Mallarmé at the end of the nineteenth century did not so much dismantle as explode traditional versification. By the twentieth century, free-form verse and the prose poem are just as common as poetry organised in stanzas.

However, even if the layout of poems changes, the emphasis on the lyrical, singing quality of poetry produced by such features as rhythm, rhyme and alliteration remains. One of the reasons why the alexandrine was so popular was that it produced a line of French that was particularly beautiful to hear. Poetry often rhymes because there is a quirky pleasure to be had from pronouncing a rhyme. Furthermore rhyme lends a coherent, finished quality to a piece of verse and can seem motivation enough for the choice of one word rather than another. Poetry in its structure (no matter how free-form) alerts us to the musicality of language, to the effects it can have beyond that of making sense. Or perhaps it is better to say that poetry makes sense on an entirely different level, using musicality to seduce, persuade and enchant a reader. Some modern poetry takes the lyric dimension of poetry to an extreme, pointing a spotlight on the poem's fascination with the sound of words. Robert Desnos's 'Élégant cantique de Salomé Salomon' (1923) is a good, if untranslatable example. This poem moves from an alliterative concentration on the consonants 'm' and 'n':

> 'Mon mal meurt mais mes mains miment
> Noeuds, neuf non anneaux. Nul nord
> Même amour mol?'

(Mourning my malady my hands mime/Knots, nerves not rings. No north nor/Malleable amours?)

to an ever more simplified insistence on the two letters:

> Aime haine
> Et n'aime
> Haine aime
> Aimai ne

(Love hate/Only love/hate love/loved hate)

> M N
> N M
> N M
> M N

It is rather as if the poem performs a striptease, hiding the consonants away within words that display only their ghostly contours, until finally they are revealed in their full glory as the motivating obsession of the poem. The structure of the poem also mimics this gradual revelation and intensification. The lines of the stanzas become ever shorter and their staggered quality has the appearance of a series of steps, leading the reader down into the heart of the poem. Although visual and phonic factors dominate this poem, we cannot dispense with the more conventional meaning of the words. It is, after all, interesting that the oscillation between 'm' and 'n' should be contained within the words for love and hate. The hopping backwards and forwards between the two consonants is endowed with an emotional quality, as if the identification of 'aime' with 'm' and 'haine' with 'n' were the discovery of a profound truth about the nature of the two letters, or a profound truth about the nature of the two emotions.

Already we can see that reading a poem draws on very different interpretative faculties to reading a novel. Poems simply do not make sense in an intellectual way; instead they require an imaginative response from the reader, and one that has as much to do with the way the words sound and their placement on the page as with their dictionary definitions. Poems are sensual experiences, provoking an emotional response through the sheer feeling of pronouncing words that are harsh or sibilant, whispering or aggressive. Certain words have a kind of natural alliance to either a major or minor key; some sound naturally flat, while others are sharp. Poems are also visual experiences, asking us to consider the look of words out of their natural context, as well as conjuring images out of the blank spaces of the page. Reading a poem requires us to use all our senses, as well as our abilities to imagine, to analyse and to fantasise, for every bit of a poem is potentially meaningful and every bit of our response to it is potentially useful.

However, if the 'meaning' of a poem is not something we can deduce intellectually, what do we actually mean by the term 'meaning'? It is perhaps easier to understand what poems do if we stop expecting them to explain. Narrative explains, but poems are more akin to pictures, which can provoke wonder or fascination but do not offer an intellectually satisfying 'answer' to the questions they pose. Perhaps it is even better to think of poems as dreams on paper where a series of intensely evocative images follow in quick succession but are missing the causal links that would help them to 'make sense'. Like dreams (and pictures) as well, poems are intensely visual, in that the reader responds emotionally to the images in a way that bypasses conventional thought. In fact, poets like Paul Éluard considered images to be most powerful when they defied the human intellect. One reasonably straightforward image we can consider occurs in Francis Picabia's 1917 poem 'Délicieux':

> Cette époque n'est qu'une femme malade –
> Laissez-la crier, tempêter, disputer,
> Laissez-lui briser table et assiettes.'

(This age is nothing but a sick woman/ Let her argue, rant and rail/ Let her smash table and plates.)

Comparing a historical era to a sick woman is intellectually difficult to do and not particularly productive. But to encapsulate the idea in a metaphor has infinitely more power. This image explains nothing, but it points in all kinds of directions towards interpretations we might like to make. We can see in this image the two ingredients in the witches' brew of poetry. The first is an evocative sample of experience, the horror, fear and fascination bound up in watching a sick woman live out her suffering; the second is an abstract notion or idea, which is harder to put your finger on, but which in this case is an implicit judgement on the historical time of writing. Given that this poem was published in 1917, we can read into it the hysteria of the First World War, both on the battlefront, amid the carnage of trench warfare, and at home, where families mourned the loss of their menfolk behind closed doors. The image is common and domestic but powerful because the violent suffering of others is always uncomfortable to witness. Also it unites people's experiences in a time when it must have seemed that the world had gone mad. So we can see how poetry is a finely balanced art, evoking impressions and emotions that are too complex or paradoxical to be expressed in the language of reason. As in dreams, we 'see' emotions and ideas that we do not logically understand but which are very much a part of our experience. Poetry, then, is a kind of witchcraft that effects the trick of making what is invisible visible, opening our eyes to the abstract, the unreal, the impossible that underlies the everyday. The effect of poetry is similar to that of hot summer sun on tarmac; it transforms the familiar landscape through its shimmering, hazy, brilliance so that we can see the invisible heat rising.

Modern French poetry has a number of strong influences affecting its development, most of which can be traced back to the early decades of the century. Perhaps the most widespread and pervasive was the general aesthetic desire of the modern age to push everything to its logical extreme. As I mentioned earlier, by the end of the nineteenth century traditional versification was not so much dismantled as exploded, and the poets of the new century were more than ready to develop the notion of a poem as organic, living, spontaneous and unpredictable. The poetry of the modern world needed to reflect the end of the belief in an ordered universe, and to embrace instead the fragmentation, alienation and sheer speed of living that was now the common experience. The poet Guillaume Apollinaire (1880-1918) is best known for capturing the sense of standing on the threshold of a new era, with all its excitements and anxieties. His poems transform the 'unpoetic' twentieth century by evoking the very dislocation of the modern sensibility, invaded by the violent and vivid sensations of city life, surrounded by a world that is no longer easy to interpret.

Apollinaire was also responsible for forging what would prove to be significant and productive links between poetry and painting. He was particularly interested in the Cubist movement which sought to reproduce the 'simultaneity' of modern life. In painting, this means that multiple points of view are represented at the same time; for instance, this is why Picasso paints the picture of Dora Maar with what looks like three noses, for he is effectively depicting her from three perspectives at once. In poetry, Apollinaire sought to reproduce this effect by frustrating the typical temporality of reading (this happened, and then this happened, and so on). Instead he represented a slice through time, exploiting the poetic potential of a single moment (see his poem 'Lundi, rue Christine' which I analyse later). Apollinaire's other well-known innovation is the picture-poem, or *calligramme*, which plays with the typography of a poem, possible now that printing practices had improved, to create pictures from words. In one simple instance, the poem 'La pluie', words fall in slanting diagonal lines, evoking pictorially as well as through the sounds of the words, the rain they represent. Apollinaire's incorporation of the white space of the paper into his poetry, his experimentation with the placement of his poems on the page to add a further visual dimension to his work, set a trend that would be explored and developed throughout the century.

Modern poetry thus seeks to revolutionise the reading experience, making it more complex and more involving for the reader. Underlying many of the special effects it uses to achieve this is the notion of juxtaposition. Juxtaposition is essential to popular artistic practices in the early twentieth century such as montage and collage, whereby pictures are created from a wide range of different and often non-artistic media such as textiles, bus tickets, newspaper clippings and café menus. In painting this worked to confuse what was reality and what was representation, as well as what was considered aesthetic and what was not. But while in the visual arts it resulted in an interesting form of experimentation, in poetry juxtaposition was increasingly understood as one of the central dynamic forces in a poem's creation. The poet Pierre Reverdy's theory of the poetic image, developed in 1918, redefines poetic practice for the modern age. Reverdy described the poetic image as the juxtaposition of two more or less distant realities, arguing that the more distant the relationship between them, the greater the power of the image. If we take the image we were discussing earlier, of the era being like a sick woman, we can see that it works through the unexpected similarity discovered in radically dissimilar notions. Because the notions are so dissimilar, there is no likelihood that we will confuse them; instead, the poetic image requires the reader to hold in his or her imagination both notions simultaneously in a relationship of both identity and difference. The relationship between them that the mind constructs, a kind of shimmering backwards and forwards between first one and then the other, allows us to see, like the heat rising off the road, the imaginary dimensions to what we had previously only considered from one perspective.

Juxtaposition within the poetic image became increasingly important in the artistic movement that followed the First World War: Surrealism. The Surrealists were profoundly influenced by the work of the psychoanalyst, Sigmund Freud. Through his analysis of phenomena such as dreams and slips of the tongue, Freud discovered the unconscious, the part of the human mind withdrawn from consciousness that contains socially unacceptable desires and instincts. The Surrealists believed that the First World War proved the failure of rationalist bourgeois culture. What was the point in people being polite and controlled and uptight if the slaughter of the trenches was the result? They decided to free modern culture from the stranglehold of rationality by restoring access to unconscious desire that reason fought to repress.

The founder members of the movement, Louis Aragon, André Breton and Philippe Soupault, sought to unleash the energy and creativity of the unconscious, with the help of drink and drugs, and thus tap into unknown and unexplored reserves of the human mind. Their beliefs were based on a misreading of Freud who had defined the unconscious as precisely that which could never be consciously reached. But in its practices of automatic writing (writing whatever comes into your mind without any censorship or organisation), exploration of dream states, and relentless creation of bizarre images, Surrealism provided such fresh artistic impetus that it dominated poetry in the interwar years. One of its founding images was by the poet Lautréamont, who declared that no sight was more evocative than the juxtaposition of an umbrella and a sewing machine on an operating table. This will give you some idea of the distance between the objects in the modern poetic image of which Reverdy speaks, and some recognition of the difficulty involved in understanding in any intellectual way the abstract idea that the image embodies. Given that poetry is an art-form that relies upon the eccentric engagement of the imagination with reality, and that seeks to create a bewitched atmosphere in which a new world of impossibilities and incongruities becomes quite natural, Surrealism seemed the perfect refinement of all that poetry aims to achieve.

The effects of Surrealism have continued to echo across the entire length of the century, interrupted briefly during the Second World War when resistance poetry became dominant, but identifiable even today in the work of contemporary poets. Some poets such as Paul Éluard (1895-1952), Réné Char (1907-88) and Henri Michaux (1899-1984) revealed the influence quite openly, while others, notably Francis Ponge, defined his work in opposition to what he saw as Surrealism's lack of restraint. Surrealism championed the wild, unfettered outpourings of the imagination central to poetic creation. Ponge, however, recognised that poetry is equally concerned with the delicate precision of word selection, and the painstaking creation of a verbal portrait that resonates with its physical counterpart. Ponge's much respected poetry, addressing the everyday world of objects such as bread and oranges, countered to some extent the excesses of surrealism. Some of the great contemporary poets like Yves Bonnefoy achieve their poetic vision through a combination of the free association and leaps of imagination derived from Surrealist practice, with the perfect verbal encapsulation of minute elements of experience, more reminiscent of Ponge.

While identifying poetic trends across the century helps create a context for reading modern poetry, individual poems can still seem to defy all frameworks of appreciation. I am now going to offer a series of commentaries that will put into practice the theory I have up until now been exploring. In these commentaries I will start with the poems that are seemingly more accessible and progress towards those that are more complex. The categories of poetry that I use are by no means comprehensive or official in any way; they simply designate my own understanding of the various kinds of impact modern poetry has on the reader. Furthermore, although I identify each poem with one category alone, it is more likely that several of the categories I mention will coexist in one poem. The readings I undertake are in no way comprehensive; they offer only guidelines to the new reader that can be developed or abandoned as he or she pleases. The beauty, and the challenge, of poetry is that there are no rules, no safety nets of interpretation, and no definitive answers. One must put aside the need to be right, and the desire to know for sure, and instead agree to submit to the powers of witchcraft that govern poetry's domains.

Poems as happenings

Guillaume Apollinaire, extract from 'Lundi, rue Christine' (Monday, rue Christine), from *Calligrammes* (1918):

Cher monsieur
Vous êtes un mec à la mie de pain
Cette dame a le nez comme un ver solitaire
Louise a oublié sa fourrure
Moi je n'ai pas de fourrure et je n'ai pas froid
Le Danois fume sa cigarette en consultant l'horaire
Le chat noir traverse la brasserie
Ces crêpes étaient exquises

La fontaine coule
Robe noire comme ses ongles
C'est complètement impossible
Voici monsieur
La bague en malachite
Le sol est semé de sciure
Alors c'est vrai
La serveuse rousse a été enlevée par un libraire

(Dear Sir
You are a useless sort of bloke
That woman has a nose like a tapeworm
Louise has forgotten her fur coat
I don't have a fur coat and I'm not cold
The Danish man smokes a cigarette and checks the time
The black cat crosses the brasserie
These crêpes were exquisite

The fountain flows
A dress as black as her nails
It's completely impossible
Here you are, Sir
The ring with a malachite stone
The floor is strewn with sawdust
So it's true
The redhaired waitress has been carried off by a bookseller)

This extract comes from a lengthy poem by Apollinaire that maintains the same tone throughout. At first glance this poem can seem
utterly incomprehensible. Each line is a self-contained fragment,

connecting to no other, providing no progression of theme or thought, utterly mysterious and inpenetrable. But the title holds a large clue. If this is Monday, and we are on the rue Christine, then we must be witnessing a street scene of some kind. The incomplete and discontinuous lines of poetry now reveal their identity as scraps of conversation or fragments of description. We are perhaps in a café, given the references to waiters and crêpes and sawdust on the floor. Outside the window (maybe) a fountain flows, and around us snippets of overheard conversation from the other customers rise and fall. This is a poem that does not seek to explain anything as it is entirely without plot. Instead it plunges us into the heart of an experience. Each little fragment is an evocative nugget of a sight or sensation, like the woman's black fingernails that match her dress, the cat making its sinuous path across the restaurant, or the hissing alliteration of a 'sol semé de sciure'. This poem, then, is the kind of condensed verbal theatre that I mentioned at the start of the chapter. It does not narrate, but presents its subject dramatically, with small, local explosions of colours, sounds, impressions. We are not asked to understand it, but to live it, to allow the phrases to transform into a sensory experience that we can see and hear and taste. We can read this poem as being the representation of a moment taken out of time and, as such, it becomes a perfect example of the Cubist simultaneity that Apollinaire was so keen to reproduce in poetry. There is no temporal dimension to this poem and so we could imagine that all these conversations are happening at once, that it portrays a slice taken *through* time rather than across it, which would account for the unfinished and inconsequential nature of its fragments.

Having come this far, we can see in retrospect that what makes this poem initially confusing is the lack of a point of orientation. There is no poet as such who tells us about the scene, and who would therefore tell us what the scene means. Instead we are struck by the anonymity of the poetic voice, by the replacement of a consciousness that experiences with unattributed snatches of dialogue and emotionally empty if evocative instances of description. If we study the vocabulary even closer we can see that there are no abstract or theoretical words, no bodiless words like 'espoir' or 'temps' or 'amour', nothing that gives us any clue as to the idea or notion that lies behind this poem. Instead the vocabulary is resolutely physical, tied to the simple and the everyday. We could perhaps read this absence of human emotion inhabiting the poetic voice as the very notion that motivates it, and recognise the historical specificity of this café scene written in the early years of the century. The new modern age brought with it rapid change in city life; cars, planes, telephones, connected people faster with one another but meant they could be more distant from one another. It was now quite possible to sit in a café, watching life pass by at disorienting speed, and be among total strangers. 'Lundi, rue Christine' records not just the flavour of Parisian café society but the new sensibility that inhabited it; the observer whose dislocation had reached such a pitch that he could record the familiar sights and remain wholly unmoved, utterly disengaged from them. In the twentieth century, anonymity had pierced even the poet's soul. This poem dramatises a new poetic voice for a new modern world.

Poems as enigmas

Yves Bonnefoy, 'La vie errante' (The Wandering Life), from *La Vie errante* (1993):

> Il s'efforçait depuis quelques jours d'être heureux des nuages qu'il amoncelait sur sa toile au-dessus d'un chemin de pierres. Mais qu'est ce que la beauté quand on sait que l'on va partir? Demain le bateau va le conduire vers une autre île. Il ne reviendra plus dans celle-ci, il ne reverra plus ce chemin.

> Il trembla d'angoisse, soudain, et laissa tomber son pinceau dont un peu de l'ocre sombre, presque du rouge, éclaboussa le bas de la toile. Ah! Quelle joie!

> Chateaubriand au bord du Jourdain après le long voyage, que peut-il faire sinon emplir une fiole de l'eau du fleuve? Il écrit sur une étiquette: eau du Jourdain.

> Tache, épiphanie de ce qui n'a pas de forme, pas de sens, tu es le don imprévu que j'emporte jalousement, laissant inachevée la vaine peinture. Tu vas m'illuminer, tu me sauves.

N'es-tu pas de ce lieu et de cet instant un fragment réel, une parcelle de l'or, là où je ne prétendais qu'au reflet qui trahit, au souvenir qui déchire? J'ai arraché un lambeau à la robe qui a échappé comme un rêve aux doigts crispés de l'enfance.

(For several days now he had been striving to take pleasure in the clouds he was banking up on the canvas above a stony path. But what use is beauty when one knows departure is imminent? Tomorrow the boat would carry him to another island. Never again would he return to this one, never again will he see this path.

He trembled with distress, suddenly, and dropped his paint-brush from which a drop of dark ochre, almost red, fell and splashed the bottom of the canvas. Oh! Such joy!

Chateaubriand on the banks of the Jordan after his long voyage, what else can he do except fill a vial with river water? He writes on a label: water from the river Jordan.

Paint splash, epiphany of that which lacks form or meaning, you are the unexpected gift that I jealously carry with me, leaving unfinished the futile painting. You will enlighten me, you save me.

Is it not true that you are a fragment of reality from this place and this time, a parcel of gold, there where I aspired to create only reflections that betray and memories that destroy. I have torn a scrap from the dress that slipped like a dream through the grasping fingers of childhood.)

All poems are enigmatic to some extent, and so this category could look rather redundant, but the Bonnefoy prose poem above is a perfect example of a poem where something has definitely happened, but it is unclear what it is, and what it means. It is a poem where an enigma is central to its motivation, but unlike some other modern poems, this one contains the clues to a certain kind of poetic unravelling.

In this poem we have five stanzas that develop an idea and effectively tell a story, but the movement between them is not clearly
causal. We notice, however, that there are certain dynamics at work,
certain currents of energy running through the poem that cause
change and metamorphosis in ways that are evident but unexplained. We can begin to pick out these dynamics as if they were
differently coloured threads in a tangled ball, recognising that they
all rely upon each other for significance. The obvious place to start
is with the poet who begins the poem melancholic but ends it transformed by joy. The transformation of the poet is marked by a shift
through a number of different voices. The poem begins with the
impersonal 'il s'efforçait', taking a view from outside the poetic consciousness. This changes after the paint is splashed to the poet's
direct address of the artwork: 'tu vas m'illuminer, tu me sauves.' By
now the poet has recovered his own self-possession and in the final
stanza reasserts his own voice in the poignant phrase, 'j'ai arraché
un lambeau…'.

Already we can see how caught up this movement is with the
transformation of the work of art. It begins as a failed painting,
which is ostensibly spoilt by the unforeseen splash of paint. But
suddenly this accident, this 'don imprévu' or 'parcelle de l'or'
saves the painting and makes it a success. Now we need to ask ourselves why the painting was so important to the poet, and again the
answer is quite straightforward; it was intended to create a souvenir for the poet, a memory of a place he has visited and loved.
When the poem opens he has realised that choosing to create such
a memory through a painting is impossible, and he is in mourning
for the island landscape before he has even left it. But in its spon-
taneity and unexpectedness the accidental splash of paint offers
the poet the 'fragment réel' he had lost hope of preserving, and at
this point he remembers another great artist, Chateaubriand,
whose bottle of water from the Jordan river performed the same
function. So we can trace another, more hidden dynamic; one that
rejects conventional representation, conventional painting as
sterile and soulless, in favour of something that is fragmentary and
abstract, but real.

Yet this splash of paint around which the poem revolves, tells us
nothing. For all its ostensible realness, it is meaningless out of con-

text. It contains all the enigma and fascination of the image in a dream, where the image is far less important than what it stands for and the impulses that have created it. In the poem the paint splash is significant because it marks the moment when a memory is created, but that memory, as Bonnefoy shows us, is about so much more than that paint. It is a memory concerning the very possibility of memory, and its preservation, or even its creation, through the work of art. The poet's relationship to memory undergoes a sea change as a result of the splash of paint. When the poem opens he is on the point of leaving the island and on the point of renouncing art, and this combination leaves him dispossessed, unable to speak with his own voice. But the splash of paint provides a hinge, a revelatory moment that switches art from representation (painting) to abstraction (paint splash), and transforms the artist from despair to salvation, from the self-alienation of 'il' to the self-possession of 'je'. So, from this we can understand that memory is most potent when it records, not the way things stay the same, but the way things change; the borderlines that are transgressed and the accidents that reveal. And what we remember is significant precisely because it highlights moments of transformation and connection in what often appears outwardly banal or meaningless.

Reaffirmed in his creative powers, the poet is free to indulge in his final, lyrical sentence, a sentence that sums up the original loss that is reawakened by all we must subsequently agree to forsake or abandon. His final phrase reaches far back through time to grasp at the most fleeting and elusive images of the past, symbolised by the mother's dress slipping through the child's fingers. This rich and evocative poetic image mobilises any number of creative points of analogy; the fragment of the dress with the fragment of the real that is the paint splash, the dream-like quality of the poem with the dream that is childhood, the elusive, longed-for mother with the inevitable losses that the passing of time occasions, the clutching hands of the child with the hand of the artist who paints or the poet who writes. Like the very best poetic images, this one points in many directions at once, encapsulating the meaning of the poem without circumscribing it, encouraging us to read creatively, to return again and again to the body of the poem while speculating beyond the words on the page.

Poems that visualise

Francis Ponge, 'La Bougie' (The Candle), from *Le Parti pris des choses* (1942):

La nuit parfois ravive une plante singulière dont la lueur décompose les chambres meublées en massifs d'ombres.

Sa feuille d'or tient impassible au creux d'une colonnette d'albâtre par un pédoncule très noir.

Les papillons miteux l'assaillent de préférence à la lune trop haute, qui vaporise les bois. Mais brûlés aussitôt ou vannés dans la bagarre, tous frémissent aux bords d'une frénésie voisine de la stupeur.

Cependent la bougie, par le vacillement des clartés sur le livre au brusque dégagement des fumées originales encourage le lecteur, – puis s'incline sur son assiette et se noie dans son aliment.

(The night sometimes revives an unusual plant whose light transforms furnished rooms into rocky outcrops of shadows. Its golden leaf stands impassive in the hollow of an alabaster column on top of a richly black peduncle. Dusty butterflies attack it in preference to the too-high moon that mists the trees. But burnt immediately or exhausted by the battle they all quiver on the edge of a frenzy that is almost a stupor. However, the candle, by the light that flickers on the book with each abrupt emission of smoke, encourages the reader – then droops onto its plate and drowns in its own substance.)

Francis Ponge notoriously wrote poetry because he had an almost neurotic inhibition about the spoken word. In coversation he was afraid he would not have sufficient time to work out what he wanted to say, with the result that his self-expression would be inaccurate and shoddy. This fear crippled him in exams, where in France the oral is a significant part of the examination system. Unsurprisingly, then, his poems are masterpieces of poetic precision; brief, but intensely evocative descriptions that animate the everyday world of objects. This is a classic example of the kind of poem in which the words seem to have been picked out with tweezers. It is also an excellent example of the way that poetry visualises differently to other art forms.

At every twist and turn of this poem's phrasing the reader is called upon to exercise their imagination, conjuring up a series of poetic images. We begin with the rocky outcrops of shadows in a room, move onto trees made misty by moonlight, a crumbling alabaster column, the stunned stupidity of moths dazed by a brilliant light, and finally the flickering light of a candle on the pages of a book. None of these images is difficult to picture and so we have quite a clear understanding of what the poem asks us to imagine. But having passed through this chain of visualisations, we realise that the candle, the ostensible focus of the poem, has been evoked only tangentially. In our mind's eye we do not see the candle, only its effect on all that typically surrounds it. Ponge once claimed that it was not his intention to imitate objects with his poems but to describe instead 'la vie des objets' (the life of objects). The most clearly identifiable properties of an object are those concerned with its function; its function is what makes it unique, what provides its *raison d'être*. Furthermore, the function of objects is what forces them into a relationship with the world that surrounds them, and this is demonstrated in poignant and lyric terms by the poem. The candle is evoked by the quality of the light it gives, magical in its transformation of the room, dangerously seductive to the moths, gentle and encouraging to the reader, while its appearance is evoked by analogy to a strange plant with a golden leaf on a black stalk, or a column of alabaster whose hard but creamy purity echoes the visual properties of wax. Ponge's poem incorporates a paradox of description, in that to perceive the specificity of an object we must consider it through analogy or metaphor, through imagining what it is not rather than what it is.

This is particularly interesting when we come to consider the final paragraph, in which the candle is delicately anthropomorphised (that is to say, attributed with human qualities). Firstly by the way it uses its light to encourage the reader, and then by its oddly suicidal gesture of drowning in its own substance. Such images give us pause for thought: by animating the humble candle this way, what effect does the poet produce? The final image of the candle is a

powerful one, and until we draw attention to it, the anthropomor-
phic description merges with the other analogies and comparisons
the poem has already created. Describing objects in human terms
comes quite naturally to us, and provides an enlightening frame of
reference, not just for picturing the object, but for seeing ourselves
reflected in it. Candles cannot encourage and they cannot drown,
but by describing them thus we put a comforting and understand-
able framework around their utterly alien and indifferent being.
Candlelight brings comfort in the darkness, so there is a logical progression to imagining the candle as benevolent and self-sacrificing.
But what this image also illuminates is our own desire for comfort,
and the faith we put in the candle to provide it.

Furthermore, the stream of descriptions this poem produces
alerts us to the implied presence of the poet. Although the poet
remains anonymous we hear the particular poetic voice speaking
through the poem nevertheless. We see the poet looking at the
candle this way and that, conjuring up the swarm of different associations that might evoke the very essence of the candle. It was
another of Ponge's contentions that man could only apprehend
himself through turning his gaze outwards to the world around him.
In this poem we see ourselves reflected in the anthropomorphised
candle, and we watch the lively creativity of the poet searching for
the essence of the candle. Ponge saw in his poetry of objects the possibility of reconciling man to a world that could at times seem
impenetrable and resistant to him, and this by means of a language
whose imperfections he would only despair unless he turned them
to his own account.

Ultimately what this poem achieves is to demonstrate the specificity of language. Ponge does not seek to find the one perfect word
that would represent the object as it truly is; language does not work
that way as Ponge proves by never using the word 'candle' beyond
the poem's title. The true witchcraft of words lies in their ability to
conjure the object up out of a disparate set of verbal ingredients, to
create a poem like a candle in the way it flickers with brilliant images
before dying with abrupt finality. In this poem Ponge deploys language to produce a piece of art that is the equivalent of the candle,
that mobilises the multiple associations we have to candles to provide a multi-faceted, living, dynamic hologram in words.

Poems that sing

Paul Éluard, 'L'Amoureuse' (Woman in love), from *L'amour, la poésie* (1929):

> Elle est debout sur mes paupières
> Et ses cheveux sont dans les miens,
> Elle a la forme de mes mains,
> Elle a la couleur de mes yeux,
> Elle s'engloutit dans mon ombre
> Comme une pierre sur le ciel.
>
> Elle a toujours les yeux ouverts
> Et ne me laisse pas dormir.
> Ses rêves en pleine lumière
> Font s'évaporer les soleils,
> Me font rire, pleurer et rire,
> Parler sans avoir rien à dire.
>
> (She is standing on my eyelids
> And her hair is in my hair,
> She has the form of my hands,
> She has the colour of my eyes,
> She is swallowed up by my shadow
> Like a stone against the sky.
>
> She always has her eyes wide open
> And she does not let me sleep.
> Her dreams in broad daylight
> Make the suns evaporate,
> Make me laugh, cry and laugh,
> Speak when I have nothing to say.)

There is a lovely moment in a novel by the decadent author, Rachilde, in which she speaks of the desire to make writing 'chanter l'idée' (sing the idea). Writing, when it is literary, goes beyond statement or explanation by incorporating another dimension of meaning that is simply bound to the beauty of its expression. There

are certain modern French poets who make their ideas sing, and
Paul Éluard is one of them. 'L'Amoureuse' is typical of Éluard's love
poetry, and perhaps the transformations wrought on the poet by the
force of love are the most naturally melodious of all lyric subjects.
This is clearly a poem that resists classic interpretation, but its
rhythms and images are so beautiful we can still appreciate it while
being utterly bewildered by what it aims to convey.

So how can we begin to appreciate this poem when it places such
impossible demands of mental visualisation upon us? The very first
line defies all our usual frames of reference. But if we remember
that one of the classic poems of love – 'my love is like a red, red
rose' – is hardly an object lesson in obvious analogies, then perhaps
we can stop feeling quite so disoriented. In this love poem, Éluard's
linguistic trick is to suggest that his love *is* a red rose. Éluard dispenses with similes and chooses figurative, metaphorical
descriptions instead. The result is more dramatic, more provocative, and just that bit harder to comprehend. If we look again at the
first five lines of the stanza, and this time as a whole, we begin to
receive an impression of the woman as a force or spirit who corre-
sponds perfectly to the poet's being, who is now filling his field of
vision, now swallowed up in his shadow. The repetition of 'elle' at
the beginning of each line adds a coherence of rhythm to the
stanza and gives it the sense of an incantation or chant. Although
the woman is the focus of attention, the poet is subtly insinuated
into her being, for his hands, his eyes, his shadow are all in perfect
correspondence to hers. The intensity of the woman's love (for the
title indicates she is the loving force) binds the two of them
together in a way that obscures their differences, making them now
entwined, now identical, now dissolved in one another. Yet the final
line of this stanza jolts the reader again with its abrupt dissonance.
The qualifying 'comme' that should clarify the relationship asks us
yet again to reconsider the relationships we have been imagining.
After a series of images where bodies merge and interconnect, the
image of a stone outlined against the sky ends the stanza on a note
of abrupt distinction.

The shock value of this simile is probably justification enough for
its existence. But if we continue reading on into the second stanza
we find a series of lines that suggest the power and the agency of the

woman. Here the woman exerts her influence over the poet, pre-
venting him from sleeping, perhaps because her wide-awake gaze
demands a response from him. In another of Éluard's rich but
taxing images we are told that her dreams make the sun evaporate,
and the qualifier 'en pleine lumière' indicates that she possesses
almost magical powers if she can bring her dreams into the light of
day and challenge the brilliance of the sun with them. There is a
sense then, that for all the woman's ability to merge with and reflect
the poet, she exerts impressive talents of her own, talents that make
her stand out, with the clarity and distinctness of a stone against the
sky. She is thus a kind of magician, or visual acrobat, appearing and
disappearing, transforming into the poet's double, filling the field
of his vision, bringing her dreams to life. Of course we could throw
our hands in the air and cry, but it doesn't make sense! Or we could
consider whether being in love ever had anything to do with making
sense, and understand that Éluard's figurative use of language
reaches out to the effects and transformations caused by love, for
which we have no sensible descriptions.

The significant use of dreams and the overall anti-rationalist
quality of the poem alerts us to the fact that Éluard was a Surrealist
poet. Another way of reading this poem is to recognise the presence
of the unconscious in its unusual forms of expression. If the conscious mind is the domain of sense, reason and order, then the
unconscious is necessarily aligned to contradiction, impossibility,
ambiguity and even meaninglessness. The playful if confusing
images of the poem can then be read as influenced by the unconscious mind, as if the poem were a beautiful, evocative but
inexplicable dream. Surrealist writers had a tendency to believe that
women possessed a special link to the unconsious, and that they
were more in tune with primal instincts and desires than men. Often
women appear in Surrealist texts as otherworldly muses, aiding and
inspiring the male artist. Occasionally this can deteriorate into a
kind of patronising reverence, but Éluard's poem avoids such pit-
falls in its genuinely entranced tone, and its teasing tenderness.

In contrast to the rest of the poem, the last two lines are not only
direct and unambiguous, but they are also spoken by the poet about
himself. We can follow up on our previous reading by understanding
this switch in tone as representing the move from the paradoxical

world of the woman, into the more rational world of the man. But in this final rhyming couplet – a perfect example of rhyme lending a finished and coherent feel to a poem – the trace of the woman is still apparent. The woman inhabits the poet where it most matters: in his poetic voice. She makes him laugh and cry, forcing him to both ends of the vocal spectrum, and she inserts meaninglessness into his speech. We could read 'parler sans avoir rien à dire' as a final subversion of the entire poem, suggesting it is not actually able to say anything of consequence. Or we could read it as an endorsement of the Surrealist project – speaking while having nothing necessarily to say is their precondition to artistic creativity after all. Or we could read that 'nothing to say' as the conclusive identification of a poem that chooses instead to sing; to laugh and cry through words, to burble and praise, and indulge in all those other speech acts where the emotion is more important than its expression. Éluard's poem seems resistant to understanding, but it does not ask us to rationalise its meaning. It is a poem that dramatises the state of blissful confusion that is being in love. Like a lover it asks only our sympathetic complicity in its madness, and our nostalgic pleasure in its siren song of desire.

Twentieth-century poetry may well be difficult to understand, but it performs the useful function of making us think differently about language and the possibilities of expression it contains. Poetry is a prime domain of linguistic experimentation, but the need to find new ways to articulate emotions and events would be a dominant theme across the diverse genres of modern French literature. The Surrealist belief that reason had lost its power in the twentieth century would hold increasing conviction amongst writers, forcing them to find alternative ways to understand the world. One of the most significant theories of modern reality, based on a complete reassessment of our understanding of reason, forms the basis of my next chapter: the theory of Existentialism.

Suggested reading

Roger Little, *The Shaping of Modern French Poetry* (Manchester: Carcanet Press, 1995). An excellent introduction to unrhymed poetry that encompasses the work of the Symbolists, Rimbaud and Mallarmé, as well as a wide range of twentieth-century poets.
Clive Scott, *Reading the Rhythm: the poetics of French Free Verse 1910-1930*

(Oxford: Clarendon Press, 1993). For those who have a particular fascination with versification, a series of detailed poetic readings of Ponge and Supervielle among others.

Tim Mathews, *Reading Apollinaire: Theories of Poetic Language* (Manchester: Manchester University Press, 1987) Sophisticated and challenging readings of the poetry, but worth the effort.

Ian Higgins, *Francis Ponge* (London: Athlone Press, 1979). The Athlone series of critical texts on poets is consistently good; accessible and rewarding to read. Higgins on Ponge is particularly well done.

Robert Nugent, *Paul Éluard* (New York: Twayne Publishers, 1974). Another strong series of readings, and a persuasive and comprehensive critique of Éluard.

Mary Ann Caws, *Yves Bonnefoy* (Boston: Twayne Publishers, 1984). A reliable critic producing a readable and sophisticated appreciation of Bonnefoy.

3

Existentialism:

The Impossible Ideal of Ethics

It is sad but undeniably true that nowadays hardly anyone in my profession is considered to be cool. Intellectuals and academics in the arts are more likely to be thought of as eccentric at best and irrelevant at worst. We can perhaps take comfort from the recognition that the relative stability of our society in recent times has meant that we have not had a pressing need to answer the big questions. Questions such as: What is the meaning of life? How should we live it? What can be done about man's fundamental hostility to man? lose their urgency in a time of peace and economic comfort. The events of 11 September 2001 have proved, if proof were needed, that such questions never really go away. As the world stands poised for another lengthy crisis we can sympathise with the position of France in the 1940s, after Europe had suffered in one brutal and damaging world war only to find itself plunged with dread and resignation into another. France was to undergo a national and political identity crisis caused by the Nazi occupation of its northern territories, and then, as the prisoners from the concentration camps began to return, the unspeakable horror of the Holocaust was gradually revealed. At this point in time, however, world events provoked a quickening in the pace of philosophical enquiry, with the urge to understand and account for what had occurred. The philosophical overhaul of existence that had begun in Europe at the turn of the century was now reaching a climactic stage. Philosophers such as Bergson and Merleau-Ponty in France and Husserl and Heidegger in Germany were exploring the most fundamental elements of man's relationship to the world, by analysing the contents, structure and significance of consciousness. How we perceive, how we experience time passing, how we remember, what it is to be aware of our being in the world, now came under rigorous and sophisticated scrutiny.

The advent of existentialism in the form of Jean-Paul Sartre's *L'Être et le néant* (Being and Nothingness), published to great acclaim in 1943, provided the culmination of these philosophical concerns. It has subsequently become one of the best-known philosophical works of the modern age, influencing generations of writers and thinkers and guaranteeing world-wide fame for its author. While it has always had as its goal the discovery of absolute certainties, French philosophy has traditionally favoured a less abstract and mathematical approach, relating itself quite naturally to literature, politics and other human sciences. Existentialism arguably achieves its impact, not just because it provides a hard-hitting philosophy of existence with implications for our ethical and political behaviour, but because Sartre dramatised his theories in a series of bestselling novels and plays. Nor was he alone in promoting the cause of existentialism. His lifetime companion, Simone de Beauvoir (whom I discuss in Chapter 5) was also a gifted philosopher and novelist, and his friend Albert Camus, whose doctrine of the Absurd is tightly bound to existentialist thought, was eventually to be awarded the Nobel prize for literature in 1958.

To the aura of their intellectual brilliance was added the fascination of their private lives: an interwoven soap opera played out in the corridors of the Sorbonne, the offices of the publisher Gallimard, and the cafés of the Saint-Germain-des-Prés area of Paris. They were friends, lovers and rivals in the midst of the Parisian elite. Sartre and Beauvoir's relationship was sexual as well as intellectual, but they were never faithful to each other. Sartre's success with women is testimony to his wit and charisma, given that he was five foot two and had a squint. Even Beauvoir described him as short and very ugly. She was nevertheless jealous of Sartre's fascination with the Algerian-born Resistance fighter, Camus, but their friendship was to be short-lived, ending in an acrimonious dispute over Marxist thought in 1952. They represented above all the epitome of intellectual glamour, black polo-necked artists dominating café society, chain-smoking their way through philosophical discussions, ready to change the world.

In fact, the brute materiality of the world and its utter resistance to man's misguided attempts to master and control it lies at the heart of the existentialist doctrine. Man is separate from the world and his existence upon it is a complete absurdity. Existentialism is a harsh doctrine because it forces us to recognise that there is no logically compelling reason for existence; we are what Sartre termed 'contingent', or more bluntly, pointless. Rather than explain the philosophy at this point it is better to turn to the texts themselves where the dramatisation of existentialist principles makes the theory far easier to grasp.

The plight of the individual

In Sartre's *La Nausée* (Nausea, 1938) the narrator Antoine Roquentin recounts in journal form the story of what would appear to be a nervous breakdown. It is in fact the revelation of a series of uncomfortable truths about his own existence. His crisis escalates rapidly from a number of small and seemingly random events. His work on the biography of the marquis de Rollebon is going badly, he picks up a pebble on the beach and is peculiarly aware of its materiality, he goes to the café in the hope of getting laid but, on finding that the proprietress has gone shopping, he is gripped by a vertiginous panic. At these times he is overwhelmed by nausea; the world trembles before his eyes and he suffers from the symptoms of profound unease. Roquentin is deeply alarmed by these small indications of what he believes to be a much more significant sea change in his relationship to the world around him. His only method of self-defence and at the same time, self-exploration, is his journal, for he is living and working alone in Bouville and thus entirely thrown back on his own resources. The fact of his alienation from others is important; as his work ceases to entertain or occupy him, Roquentin has nothing that could distract him from the business of existing in its simplest form. But simplicity or harmony is far from what he experiences. Instead his perception of the world around him becomes unstable as objects are disengaged from their usual frames of reference.

In one attack of existential angst as he travels on the tram, the seat in front of him metamorphoses in a kind of hallucination: 'Ça pourrait tout aussi bien être un âne mort, par exemple, ballonné par l'eau et qui flotte à la dérive, le ventre en l'air dans un grand fleuve gris' (It could equally well be a dead donkey, for instance, swollen with water and floating aimlessly, its belly in the air, down a wide, grey river). Repetition of the word 'banquette' (seat) does nothing to control his frightening perceptions and Roquentin is forced to conclude that: 'Les choses se sont délivrées de leurs noms [...] je suis au milieu des Choses, les innommables. Seul, sans mots, sans défenses, elles m'environnent, sous moi, derrière moi, au-dessus de moi. Elles n'exigent rien, elles ne s'imposent pas: elles sont là.' (Objects have been delivered from their names [...] I am in the middle of Objects and they cannot be named. Alone, without words or defences, they surround me, they are underneath me, behind me, above me. They demand nothing, they make no claim on me: they are just there.) What Roquentin is experiencing is a revolution in his relationship to objects. Whereas previously it sufficed to name them to keep them in their place, now objects refuse to be so imperiously designated. Instead they threaten to overwhelm him with their stubborn physical presence. Language proves to be a fragile barrier between Roquentin and the external world, failing to refer to objects and thus place them in a scheme of meaning. Once language collapses it becomes evident that words also give a measure of control and superiority to the speaker by keeping the world at bay; when they fail in this function Roquentin is instantly vulnerable, unprotected. Surrounded by objects, Roquentin is on the point of feeling invaded, his identity compromised, except that the objects are utterly indifferent to him. But of course they are, one might say. They are objects, lumpen and unfeeling and utterly meaningless. Yet mankind fondly imagines that objects *do* have a meaning. Seats are made to be sat on, for instance. But the moment they start metamorphosing into dead donkeys is the moment when we realise that, liberated from their imposed purpose, their materiality rears up in all its ungovernable absurdity. Things become disordered, monstrous, ridiculous; what Roquentin terms 'nues, d'une effrayante et obscène nudité' (naked, with a terrifying and obscene nudity), as if language clothed disorder and made it respectable.

The bodily imagery is interesting, for Roquentin's own body has equally become objectified in his new, alarming perception. Studying his hands during a particularly sterile session in the library, he is aware, as if for the first time, of their almost autonomous existence: 'Je sens ma main. C'est moi, ces deux bêtes qui s'agitent au bout de mes bras. Ma main gratte une de ses pattes avec l'ongle d'une autre patte; je sens son poids sur la table qui n'est pas moi. [...] À la longue c'est intolérable... Je retire ma main, je la mets

3. Existentialism   63

dans ma poche. Mais je sens tout de suite, à travers l'étoffe, la chaleur de ma cuisse' (I feel my hand. This is me, these two animals agitating on the ends of my arms. My hand scratches one paw with the nails of the other paw; I feel its weight on the table which is not part of me [...] Eventually it becomes unbearable... I take my hand away and put it in my pocket. But immediately I feel, through the cloth, the warmth of my thigh). Roquentin's problem is a heightened and sensitised perception of his own fleshy existence, and this awareness – or nausea – refuses to leave him. Now that he has lifted the flimsy veil of language and lost his unthinking relation to his body, once he has seen the world for what it is (what he calls 'de trop' or excessive) he cannot return to his state of innocence.

Those readers frustrated with his introspection ('Why can't he just get a job?') miss the philosophical point. Roquentin is eyeball to eyeball with existence, with its absurd, amorphous, obstinate thereness. He knows that man's attempts to give his life meaning, or to order and understand the world, are like a fragile web woven around, but never actually touching, the indifferent matter of the universe. Our thoughts and feelings, our notions of causality and reason, our hope and fears, belong on an entirely separate plane to the physical presence of the world. It is as if human civilisation were a long dream, and Roquentin has just woken up.

This is the essential discovery of *La Nausée,* and the shift in perspective that Roquentin undergoes has far-reaching consequences. This is a philosophy that dispenses with the past and the future (products of our memory or imagination and utterly irrelevant in a life that is essentially absurd and meaningless), casting its subjects into the continual present of existence. It also dispenses with any kind of essence to identity – we are nothing more than bodies with a consciousness that is filled at any given moment with the objects that surround us. And it also dispenses with any kind of fixed value system; there is no such thing as a divine order to the universe (God is clearly a logical impossibility), so values are purely arbitrary and subjective. Given that we have no essence, and that there are no inbuilt values, man is an empty shell, totally undetermined and totally free. Man's freedom is inescapable and brings with it absolute responsibility. Nothing makes us act the way we do, except our own personal choice. This means effectively that there are no excuses; if we are greedy or selfish or unkind, we are not 'made that way' or 'unable to behave differently'. We have made a choice somewhere along the line, and then chosen to forget it.

The best example of a man made to realise his absolute freedom is Meursault in Albert Camus's *L'Étranger*, a fascinating and provocative counterpoint to Sartre's tortured hero, Roquentin. Whereas Roquentin struggles to come to terms with the absurdity of existence, feeling nauseous disgust at his lack of differentiation from the physical world around him, Meursault is a born existentialist, deriving a sensuous pleasure from the natural elements and contentedly oblivious to the search for transcendent meaning. There is nothing but the continuous present for Meursault. Each day brings the pleasure of swimming in the sea, or enjoying the heat of the sun, or the happiness of experiencing a fresh roller-towel in the toilets at his office. Meursault needs nothing more than this, which results in a gentle indifference to the people who are near him. When his girlfriend, Marie, asks if he loves her, he replies that he does not know what the word means. The opening lines of the novel: 'Aujourd'hui, maman est morte. Ou peut-être hier, je ne sais pas' (Today my mother died. Or perhaps yesterday, I don't know) are famous for their offhand imprecision. Camus carefully maintains the ambiguity of Meursault's feelings. He is by no means a heartless monster but a man to whom moral conventions are entirely alien, the property of a society that insists they are natural while imposing such behavioural constraints. Meursault is not a rebellious hero, refusing to conform to the laws of sentimentality. He simply exists.

This is all well and good, until Meursault commits an act that demands society try and reclaim him. A series of chance events involves him and his dodgy friend, Raymond, in a tussle with a group of Arabs. Raymond is hurt and persuaded to go home, leaving Meursault with his revolver. Walking aimlessly back along the beach, suffering physically from the intensity of the sun, Meursault finds himself face to face with one of the Arabs. A standoff ensues in the intolerable heat and light, and the language of the text, which up until this point has been faultlessly neutral, explodes in a series of metaphors. Meursault describes how 'son image dansait devant mes yeux dans l'air enflammé' (its image danced before my eyes in the flaming air), until 'le ciel s'ouvrait sur toute son étendue pour laisser pleuvoir du feu' (the sky split across its expanse, letting fire fall like rain). In this moment of extreme discomfort he shoots. Then he shoots four more times.

Later on, in prison, Meursault will say he killed the Arab 'à cause du soleil' (because of the sun). Naturally the lawyer, the priest and all the officials bound up in such a judicial investigation will not believe him. Readers and critics alike have been tempted not to believe him, but this is an irredeemably 'wild' act, an event that resists incorporation into any system of justification or logic. Camus's genius is to represent the murder of an innocent man as meaningless, demonstrating how hard it is not to be tempted to find some kind of explanation for an act that threatens the basis of society. Particularly when it comes within a novel, a form that generally seeks to create meaning rather than deny it. Instead, around the still, violent centre of the text, we watch a series of justificatory discourses employed in order to recuperate the act and classify Meursault.

The lawyer seeks to create a tragic hero out of Meursault, suggesting that grief for his mother altered the balance of his mind. Meursault can offer no stronger formulation than that he would have preferred his mother not to die. The examining magistrate demands that Meursault repent his act, but when asked if he regrets it, Meursault, bored and wearied by interminable discussions, replies: 'plutôt que du regret véritable, j'éprouvais un certain ennui' (rather than true regret I felt a certain annoyance). By now the flat, impersonal tone of Meursault's narrative voice, so alienating and even puzzling to the reader initially, begins to throw into relief the emotive discourses of these officials. In contrast to the cool precision of Meursault's vocabulary, the misplaced Christian dogma they preach at him, with its insistence on faith and repentence, seems laden with unnecessary sentiment and delivered with excessive vehemence. Meursault, unheroically but doggedly, is sticking by the truth, however unpalatable it may be. His refusal to allow the events of the murder to be reconfigured into a morally acceptable narrative lead to his ultimate condemnation. In court he is given the death sentence in a case that rests heavily on his apparently uncaring behaviour after his mother's death. At this point the reader, who didn't much like Meursault to begin with either, and who has had to accept the absurdity of the murder, is outraged by the injustice of the legal system and the moral pretensions on which it is constructed. Meursault's struggle to avoid misrepresentation, and his suspicion of the discourses that distort experience, start to cohere into a unique moral perspective. Even the empty tone of his narrative begins to reveal a discerning intelligence that recognises the precious weight of each word. He faces his fate with characteristic lucidity: 'Eh bien, je mourrai donc' (Oh well, then I'll die), but even Meursault cannot quite pass unthinkingly through his final hours.

Struggling to reconcile himself to death in the few hours that remain, Meursault reluctantly allows the prison chaplain to see him. But this man's obstinate insistence on the idea of heaven releases a wave of anger and resistence in Meursault. When the chaplain demands his image of the afterlife, Meursault cries out: 'Une vie où je pourrais me souvenir de celle-ci' (A life in which I can remember this one). This truth constitutes a moment of revelation for him. Meursault acknowledges that he has remained authentic, his freedom uncompromised, his truths upheld, his experience undistorted. He recognises his guilt in the eyes of society, the injustice that he has suffered, the arbitrariness of a value system he does not share, and he still loves life. In a moment of extreme poignancy he declares: 'je m'ouvrais pour la première fois à la tendre indifférence du monde' (I opened myself for the first time to the tender indifference of the world). Meursault chooses and affirms a *modus vivendi* that he has previously lived instinctively. Life is absurd and frequently fraught with contradiction, and it is the only life we have. Such tensions do not diminish the value of life, rather they render it more precious than ever.

It is impossible not to be moved by the ending of *L'Étranger*, just as it is difficult not to become caught up in Roquentin's alarming new perspective (certainly for those of us who have sat for too long in libraries). But there is a problem with these texts that centres on the extreme isolation and individuality of the narrators. For texts that focus on the revelation of a general truth of existence, and that seek to represent a more authentic underlying reality, they do not offer lifestyles with which we can identify. Are we supposed to 'be' like Meursault, who is portrayed as an aberration in society? He has, after all, committed a murder. Or are we all Roquentins under the surface, simply requiring the context of alienation to come out of the existential closet? And although love of life may be celebrated, there is very little love for others in these novels. In fact, hostility and fear are more characteristic of human relationships, and this is a feature of a number of existential texts.

Hell is other people

Sartre's play *Huis clos* was the first play performed in liberated Paris in 1944. It opened to great acclaim and quickly became one of the most popular plays of the generation. Sartre dramatises a highly particular vision of Hell – a bourgeois drawing-room in which three people are trapped for all eternity: Garcin, the intellectual shot for refusing to fight in the war, Inès the lesbian, and Estelle, the shallow but beautiful representative of the *haute bourgeoisie*. Although strangers to one another when they first arrive, it quickly becomes clear that 'Le bourreau, c'est chacun de nous pour les deux autres' (Each one of us is the torturer for the other two). Initially they have difficulty accepting their status, offering a version of their deaths that attempts to cast them in a good light. But already tensions begin to mount. Inès, the most clear-sighted, aggressive and subversive of the three, will not let such feeble self-delusion pass: 'Nous sommes en enfer, ma petite, il n'y a jamais d'erreur et on ne damne jamais les gens pour rien' (We are in hell, my dear, and there are never any mistakes and no one is damned without reason). The play proceeds to stage a series of gradual revelations in which the truth of their crimes becomes apparent, and the ways in which they will make each other suffer become clear.

Estelle, who has driven one lover to suicide and killed her baby, is the first to notice that there are no mirrors in hell (typically she wants to redo her lipstick). She declares: 'quand je ne me vois pas, j'ai beau me tâter, je me demande si j'existe pour de vrai'(When I can't see myself, even if I pinch myself, I start to wonder if I really do exist). Her need for others to reflect back to her a pleasing self-image is a weakness that Sartre suggests we all share. But Estelle requires more than admiration, she wants the other's desire and, as Sartre states in *L'Être et le néant*, 'Desire is defined as trouble'. Inès, killed by her despairing lover, desires Estelle but Estelle has no interest in a lesbian, and is in fact revolted by her. Garcin, whose love she does seek, has been caught trying to escape over the frontier and executed in dishonour. He longs for someone to reassure him that he is not a coward, and Estelle, eager to win him over, is more than prepared to do this. However, Inès realises the chance to avenge her frustration, rightly pointing out the hollowness of Estelle's declarations: 'elle te dirait que tu es Dieu le Père, si cela pouvait te faire plaisir' (She would say you were God the Father if it would please you). Thus the desires of all three are thwarted. Rather than the comfort of an acceptable self-image, the truth of their weaknesses and crimes constitutes their sole reflection.

Tension mounts to fever pitch between them, yet when the door to their room unexpectedly opens, no one is able to leave and face the unknown that lies beyond. Inès ironically comments: 'C'est à mourir de rire. Nous sommes inséparables' (You could die laughing. We are inseparable). Inseparable, partly because of an obstinate need to convince each other of their good qualities, and partly out of a lack of courage to confront a situation that could be even worse. Hell is other people, Garcin declares, but the particular poignancy of such a hell is that it is too tolerable: 'plutôt le fouet, plutôt le vitriol, que cette souffrance de tête, ce fantôme de souffrance, qui frôle, qui caresse et qui ne fait jamais assez mal' (rather the whip, rather the poison, than this imaginary suffering, this ghost of suffering which strokes and caresses and never hurts enough). It is perhaps the particular fear of a philosopher, but for Sartre it is the liminal, undecidable states that torment human beings who long for certainty. Roquentin could not bear the uncertain status of objects, and now Garcin desires the unequivocal pain of physical torture, rather than the long drawn-out agony of an afterlife that intensifies the dissatisfactions of the life he just left. Yet he lacks the strength to recognise his freedom and leave by the open door. He ends the play with the statement: 'Eh bien, continuons' (Oh well, let's continue).

The play dramatises a number of Sartre's philosophical beliefs, not least the belief that we are totally free and totally responsible. There are no excuses for the behaviour of the characters in *Huis clos*, and little evidence that they wish to change their ways. Instead their moral cowardice results in pathetic attempts to dissemble, or to disguise the crimes they have committed. Their punishment relates directly to what they have done, however, with no account taken of their regrets or unfulfilled ambitions. The existentialist moral rule is harsh and unbending. Inès voices it (and is frequently the mouth-piece of existential thought) when she tells Garcin: 'Seuls les actes décident de ce qu'on a voulu' (Acts alone determine what one intended). Lacking essence, as Sartre believes, we are the sum of our acts and nothing more. If we fail to recognise this truth, we are living in what he termed *mauvaise foi* (bad faith), a state where we prefer to discredit or ignore the harsh reality that we choose our lives.

Existence for Sartre is dynamic and at every given moment we are faced with a number of choices of how to act and thus, by extension, how to define ourselves. Even though Sartre recognises certain con-straints, he insists that we are never without choice; even a failure to act is a choice in itself. The individual suffering from *mauvaise foi* (like the characters in *Huis clos*) either pretends he has no choice, or refuses to take responsibility for his choice, revealing denial or self-delusion. This situation is further complicated in *Huis clos* by the rather bleak view of human relations that Sartre espouses. He argues in *L'Être et le néant* that all human relationships are based on conflict. This is because we seek objective recognition of our self-worth from other people. But the fact that we are all seeking the same thing means that we are all, at the same time, refusing to give that recognition to others. The result is a continual, tense stalemate. If two people do succeed in making a pact to mutually recognise each other, a third person will disrupt this balance – as Inès disrupts the tentative agreement between Garcin and Estelle.

While superficially the play would seem a perfect dramatisation of Sartre's thought, there are some philosophical problems. The first is the interesting fascination with issues of salvation and damnation from a philosopher whose thesis rests on the absence of God. It is intriguing that Sartre should set the play in hell when he argued that there was no afterlife in which such judgement could be made. Even if we claim that, as Inès suggests, 'ils ont réalisé une économie de personnel' (they have economised resources) by putting the three together to torture each other in a way that denies the necessity of God, this does not account for the mysterious 'ils' who have preordained their grouping. 'Je vous dis que tout était prévu' (I tell you that everything has been foreseen), Garcin tells the women. But by whom? And for what pur-pose? Indeed, the moral dimension of the play becomes its most problematic area. Garcin, Estelle and Inès must suffer because they are morally corrupt, but are we to consider this a kind of icing on the cake, when Sartre's theory insists that hell is other people whether they are criminals or not? Put another way, can Sartre conceive of a heaven, where people who had accumulated nothing but positive acts could go, and what would it be like? A café where one sat alone?

Issues of guilt, judgement and salvation abound in existentialist texts, reflecting the profound desire of their authors to address pertinent ethical questions. But rarely if ever do they offer a solution or provide a successful moral framework. Often they succeed only in clouding the issues beyond hope. One such text is Camus's brilliant but complex *récit, La Chute* (The Fall). In it Jean-Baptiste Clamence, ex-Parisian lawyer, sits in a sordid bar in Amsterdam, waiting to lure unsuspecting strangers into a conversation that will change their lives. One such stranger enters the bar, an anonymous silent interlocutor for Clamence. We readers, looking over his shoulder, are obliquely addressed too. Clamence tells us the story of his young life, which is that of a man who can do no wrong. He is successful in his career, lucky in love, and overflowing with virtue, or at least that is how it would seem. Clamence acts as a lawyer for the underdogs of the world, often undercharging them, while ensuring in his free time that the old and the disabled are safely escorted across the road. This continues, until one night on a bridge over the river Seine, he notices a young woman standing staring at the river. Once Clamence has passed her he hears the sound of a cry and a splash. He pauses, but keeps on walking, telling no one and making sure that he does not read the papers the following day.

This story is finally recounted in the middle of the narrative, but the reader has long been aware that some trauma has profoundly affected him. Firstly, long digressions both anticipate and defer the telling of the fall. Secondly there is the disembodied, hallucinatory laughter he hears, a sign not of happiness but of paranoia and mockery. More subtly still, we receive this impression from the ironic tone Clamence takes when describing himself. Unlike the reticent Meursault, Clamence is a king of rhetoric, but his fluent and articulate tale recalls the balance and harmony of classical French discourse only to express paradox, ambiguity and contradiction. Most of these paradoxes concern truths of human nature, deduced from his own conduct. For example, he declares: 'Il me fallait être maître de mes libéralités' (It was necessary to me to be the master of my liberalities). This is a stylishly manipulated phrase that works to expose the duplicity at the heart of human virtue. Duplicity is Clamence's main theme which he pursues obsessively. The problem is that: 'L'homme est ainsi, cher monsieur, il a deux faces: il ne peut pas aimer sans s'aimer' (That's the way man is, my dear fellow. He has two faces: he cannot love without loving himself). The result is that all good actions are contaminated to some degree by self-satisfaction. Hence in Clamence's reassessment of his former life he perceives that he was a model of virtue simply because he was a monster of vanity. All his acts of kindness or charity were motivated by smug self-righteousness and a desire to be superior to others. His brutally lucid self-examination has the result that: ' J'ai compris alors, à force de fouiller dans ma mémoire, que la modestie m'aider à briller, l'humilité à vaincre et la vertu à opprimer' (I came to understand, after searching through my memory, that modesty helped me to shine, humility to conquer, and virtue to oppress). If we believe Clamence, and he puts forward a subtly disquieting case, then the hope of a human ethics becomes a frustrating impossibility. So much for Sartre's belief that we are the sum of our acts when Clamence is suggesting that no act is ever attributable to the side of virtue or justice.

This may seem an unnecessarily harsh judgement, but Clamence's argument is carefully set up. The woman's fall from a bridge in Paris is at the same time the start of Clamence's fall from innocence to guilt. Once this incident has revealed the cowardice at the heart of his virtue he can never be wholly virtuous again. Just as one drop of ink colours a whole jug of water, so the missed encounter contaminates his conscience. This is a text steeped in a warped and fragmented form of Christian symbolism that is too complex in its associations to analyse here, but one point is clear: in the absence of God there can be no forgiveness. Man is imperfect, irredeemable, culpable, and abandoned to the summary justice of his fellow men. Such justice, far from being divine, is dominated by suspicion and doubt: 'Il y a toujours des raisons au meutre d'un homme. Il est, au contraire, impossible de justifier qu'il vive' (There are always good reasons to kill a man. It is, however, impossible to justify his existence) Clamence argues. These black and pessimistic ethics make a true judgement impossible, and yet judgement is the one certainty in an otherwise ambiguous universe. For this reason Clamence becomes a 'juge-pénitent' (judge-penitent), a man who judges himself with the utmost severity only to hold the portrait up as a mirror to his interlocutor. Clamence thus assures himself of a kind of diabolical divinity in the hell of Amsterdam: 'refugié dans un désert de pierres, de brumes et d'eaux pourries, prophète vide pour temps médiocres' (taking refuge in a wilderness of stones, fog and stagnant waters, an empty prophet in a time of mediocrity).

The historical specificity is important here. Clamence's vision of exile in the wilderness is profoundly linked to its post-Holocaust context. Clamence is a man of his time in the way that he uses mental agility and cunning, ambiguity and ambivalence, in place of truth and justice. He is profoundly disillusioned with his egotistic, solipsistic self that he has no hope of redeeming. The disordered fragments of religion that he manipulates are entirely appropriate to his crumbling, distorted ethics. As the text progresses, he falls not just from grace to guilt, but from health to sickness and from lucidity to madness. But what does it matter if Clamence is mad? The narrative persuades us that madness is an appropriate way of representing the truth in the middle of the twentieth century when the belief in man's powers of reason is at an all-time low. What does it matter, Clamence asks us, whether his stories are true or false so long as they are significant in some way? Truth is blinding, he tells us, whereas: 'Le mensonge, au contraire, est un beau crépuscule, qui met chaque objet en valeur' (Falsehood, by contrast, is a beautiful twilight that enhances every object). Clamence's world of reversal, duplicity and ambiguity is studded with examples that have a link to the Holocaust, and more than one critic has seen in Clamence's failure to witness the suicidal fall of the young woman, the difficulty of witnessing war traumas like the death camps. This is a highly particular reading of the text, but we can nevertheless deduce from Clamence's perversity a historical crisis in the possibility of ethics and a degraded, pessimistic view of man and his ability to do good.

The spirit of commitment

Existentialist thinking has a fraught relationship to the question of ethics. At its most philosophical it recognises that values are arbitrary and subjective and that there can be no demonstrable rational basis to any given value system. Yet its fundamental concern is with how we live, how we behave and what we decide to do with our lives. Hence the literary texts are shot through with fault lines of tension over questions of judgement, responsibility and guilt. This tension is also a result of the existential marriage between philosophical and literary writing. Philosophy seeks to uncover absolutes and certainties whereas literature thrives on conflict, paradox and ambiguity. When put together, the result is *littérature engagée*, literature committed to the representation of a certain world view or politics, but one that remains scrupulously honest, authentic and questioning. In the last two texts I will discuss in this section, Sartre and Camus turn their attention to the possibility of collective activity. The political face of existentialism celebrates the repression of individual desires and favours commitment to the common cause, echoing the ideology of Marxism that was popular among French intellectuals in the post-war years. Yet it is instantly apparent, having considered texts in which the isolated status of the individual and the fundamental hostility between people has taken centre stage, that such commitment to the collectivity is no easy matter.

Sartre's 1948 play, *Les Mains sales*, is arguably his finest dramatic work, if not his greatest literary achievement. Like so many other existentialist texts, its concern is the judgement of a crime, but in this case, what has motivated it, rather than what its consequences are. The play focuses on the young intellectual, Hugo, a new recruit to the Communist party in the fictional, revolution-torn country of Illyria. More from a desire to shake off his bourgeois origins than from authentic revolutionary zeal, Hugo is desperate for political action. He wants to prove his commitment to the party by risking his life for his political ideals. After much pleading, he is reluctantly trusted with the assassination of the party leader, Hoederer, who is suspected of colluding with the opposition parties. Hugo moves in as Hoederer's new secretary, taking his wife, Jessica, with him.

Now, shooting Hoederer was never going to be an easy task for the introspective, prevaricating Hugo, struggling under his burden of bad faith, believing he can be a revolutionary when he is utterly unsuited to such a role. His longing for a political ideal to which he can commit himself turns out to be a bitter response to the disillusionments of his past. When Hoederer accuses him: 'Tu n'aimes pas les hommes, Hugo, tu n'aimes que les principes', Hugo retorts: 'Les hommes? Pourquoi les aimerais-je? Est-ce qu'ils m'aiment?' ('You don't love men, Hugo, you only love principles.' Hugo: Men? Why should I love them? Do they love me?). Hugo's seething resentment says it all. While he may admire political principles, his entry into the party is more bound up with the self-serving desire to destroy his detested self-image (middle-class intellectual) and replace it with an acceptable one (heroic man of action). But we cannot simply dislike Hugo; the shame he feels for his privileged background is all too human. When he describes how, as a child, he was coaxed and cajoled into eating, self-loathing seeps from his every word. Hugo suffers from always being displaced, failing to fit in to either the life he was born with or the new life he has chosen. Surrounded by communists who entered the party through dire economic necessity, Hugo pits himself against people utterly unable to sympathise with his inferiority complex. But Hugo's mistake is to blame other people for his situation. He blames first his family and then the party, reproaching them for lack of confidence in him while he dithers and procrastinates, unable to accomplish the fateful deed.

One of the reasons why he cannot shoot Hoederer is the fact that he is increasingly drawn to him. In Hoederer Sartre created a man totally unlike his usual breed of flawed intellectuals. Hoederer is a true hero; a man of compassion and integrity, a brilliant political mind, a convincing leader, a man of courage and insight. Both Hugo and Jessica are fascinated by his ability to bring the world around him into sharp focus, to make things real. Hoederer is indeed collaborating with the opposition parties but only to negotiate as big a share of the post-revolution power for his party as possible. For Hoederer, ends justify means; he is prepared to dispense with abstract political ideals in order to achieve tangible success for the party. Hugo is forced into ever greater denial. He must ignore his attraction to Hoederer and refuse to let himself be persuaded by his arguments, in order to cling to his political purity and the hope, ever receding, that he might manage to kill him. Into this already difficult situation comes Hugo's wife, Jessica. If proof were ever needed that women come off poorly in existential texts, Jessica provides it. Intelligent, courageous and far more suited to

political action than her husband, Jessica suffers from being confined in her role as the negligible sex object. She cannot help but
meddle. While her intention to save Hugo from himself is good,
alerting Hoederer to the plan and thus allowing him to talk Hugo
out of it, her sexual attraction to Hoederer is disastrous. Just as
Hugo is reconciled to working with Hoederer and finding in him
the father figure he has always lacked, he returns to the study to find
Jessica and Hoederer embracing. Finally he shoots and Hoederer is
fatally wounded.

The story is told in retrospect and the play begins with Hugo out
of jail, returning to see Olga, a party member on whom he was
always emotionally dependent. His aim is to try to uncover the
actual motivation for his crime. He has reached the unsatisfactory
conclusion that: 'ce n'est pas moi qui ai tué, c'est le hasard' (it
wasn't me who killed him, it was chance). While this is reminiscent
of Meursault's crime 'à cause du soleil' (because of the sun), here
there are too many motivations rather than too few, and the issue in
question is not the integrity of the judicial process, but the bad faith
of the protagonist. Hugo wants to own the act but cannot do so. He
wants to believe he killed for the purity of his principles, but he
knows that emotion clouded his actions. When he finds out that in
his absence the party has changed its line and is now involved in the
collaboration that Hoederer initiated, Hugo's hope for political
purity collapses. When he finds out that Hoederer has been reha-
bilitated as a hero assassinated by the enemy, his hope of having
committed a glorious act of revolution dies as well. Knowing that
there are gunmen from the party waiting for him outside Olga's
apartment, he makes a final suicidal act of surrender to them. Hugo
hopes in this way to die heroically for his cause. He is refusing what
the party has become, refusing to deny the importance of his assassination of Hoederer, and remaining true to the political ideals of
purity he originally defended. Yet one could also read into this act
the longing for self-annihilation that has characterised Hugo's
behaviour, and a childish desire to be right, in the face of all opposition.

The play thus highlights the difficulty of sustaining abstract political ideals on a long-term basis, when political situations are always
dynamic and unstable. Yet of course any political party is founded

on a set of principles and strategies that are upheld as being the right ones, no matter what the situation. Sartre pushes this contradiction to the extreme by considering a communist party in the midst of a revolution, a party with extremely clear principles in a situation where there are no longer any rules. Reading the play today, with communism a distant memory, Hoederer's pragmatism seems far more persuasive than Hugo's naïve idealism. At the time of its performance, however, Marxism was in vogue with French intellectuals, Sartre himself was committed to the Communist party, and the ambiguity surrounding Hoederer's assassination meant that Sartre had to fight hard against an anti-Communist interpretation of his play.

In fact, we can see another reading emerge if we focus our attention on the trouble Hugo suffers trying to understand his motivation at the moment he shot Hoederer. Rather than a political crime, Hugo is committing an existential crime. While the former concerns the assassination of Hoederer, the latter concerns Hugo's relationship to his own acts. The critic Philip Thody points out that in Sartre's philosophy any act remains ambiguous and free from meaning until we choose what meaning to assign to it. The act, like all other aspects of the physical world, has no essential, pre-given significance. Hugo makes a big mistake in believing that this one crucial act will define him and confer upon him the substance he lacks. In existential terms we are never free from the responsibility to choose our lives and endlessly to redefine ourselves. Politically, Hugo may not be wrong, but existentially he makes his life a misery. For Sartre, however, it would not be the first time that the dramatic impact of his plays had worked against him, resulting in an interpretation that he never intended. His play *Bariona* was written and performed in 1940 in his prisoner-of-war camp, with Sartre among the cast. His performance was so inspiring that it led one member of the audience to convert to Christianity. The play, however, was intended to be anti-Christian in nature. If, as Hugo finds out, acts are hard to own, works of literature are even harder.

As we might have come to expect by now, ambiguity of meaning is written into the heart of Camus's text, *La Peste* (The Plague). Oran is a town on the Algerian coast that seems, when the narrative begins, to be entirely without character: 'Cette cité sans pittoresque, sans végétation et sans âme finit par sembler reposante, on s'y endort enfin' (This city without beauty, without greenery, without soul, ultimately seems peaceful; at least one slumbers there). Featureless Oran is not a town to draw attention to itself and then again, following Camus's ambivalent logic, it is precisely the sort of town that needs to be awakened from its banal and unreflective slumber. It is about to suffer as never before in the grip of a plague that will destroy its population and isolate it from the rest of the country, imprisoning its inhabitants with their fear and their grief. Describing the plot of *La Peste* can result in a rather misleading representation of the narrative. Although the story focusses on Dr Rieux and his struggle against the might of the plague, it has nothing of the Hollywood epic about it. While it remains a gripping tale of a plague-stricken town, it has none of the glamour, adventure or heroism that we have come to associate with the disaster movie. Most interestingly, for the context of this analysis, it does not have a straightforward moral framework which rewards those with the courage to fight and dispenses with the passive, the weak and the evil. Camus's plague is far more subtle and challenging than that.

Dr Rieux is as close as we come to a hero, but the point of a hero, generally, is his superiority. Heroes rejoice in having superior courage, or better knowledge. But the effect of the plague is to destroy all hierarchies of power and all sense of individuality. What the people of Oran painfully learn is that the plague is 'l'affaire de tous' (everyone's business) and that while it rages, all previous hopes and desires are irrelevant. The plague forces the townspeople into a coalition that is uneasy but unwaveringly focused on the present moment. If Rieux is a hero, it is because he recognises immediately that he must fight the plague on its own terms. What this means is that he refuses to assign any meaning to the plague. It is not a judgement on the people of Oran, and he will not be drawn into assigning a lesson or moral to their suffering. Nor will he predict the progression of the plague or waste his energies on unnecessary compassion for the dying. While this may initially make him seem cold and distant, his constant repetition that he must do his job, and the way he channels his entire energy into the often thankless task of caring for the sick, confers a kind of nobility upon his self-effacement. Rieux recognises that concerns and anxieties

beyond the immediate bounds of his role are misplaced and ultimately self-indulgent. His quiet devotion to duty eventually wins him
dignity and authenticity.

Yet in some ways, Rieux combines the emotional disinterest of
Meursault and the two faces of Clamence. For, as he admits at the
end of the narrative, he has been the anonymous narrator of the
chronicle all along. This is not necessarily a surprise; the cool, dis-
passionate tone of the narrative has always been reminiscent of
Rieux. But the narrative contains the overview that Rieux refuses
himself: 'on ne peut pas en même temps guerir et savoir' (one
cannot simultaneously care for the sick and be in the know). It is as
if the roles of narrator and doctor are necessarily so different in
relation to the plague that they must be kept apart for fear of cont-
aminating each other. This is interesting, in a text where
contamination is rife. The doctor must keep focused on the level of
the individual patient, preferring the official statistics to give him
knowledge of the plague rather than a description that would give it
a symbolic identity. By contrast the narrator is quietly omniscient,
and poetically insightful, aware at all times of the 'general' response
of the town's citizens: 'Cette ville déserte [...] gémissait alors
comme une île malheureuse' (The deserted town was keening like
an unhappy island), and even admiring the might of the plague with
its its 'éfficacité mathématique et souveraine' (mathematical and
masterful efficiency).

This admiration for what should be abhorred reveals the typical
ambiguity in Camus's text. The plague is not simply bad, for it tem-
porarily forces the inhabitants of Oran into an acute self-awareness.
It reveals the fragility and beauty of life, reawakening love and desire
in those who have been separated, demanding a new level of understanding of existence, and creating a community of committed
individuals who learn to fight together. The team that Rieux builds
includes men like the journalist Rambert, who makes several aborted
attempts to escape from the town before deciding to stay and help in
any way he can. The community is not perfect, and it in no way
replaces or transcends individual desires, but within the constraints
imposed by the plague, it does at least offer some consolation.

The sense of community extends to the narrative voice itself
which includes reports and testimonies from other observers,

notably Jean Tarrou whose notebooks provide a very different perspective on the outbreak. Tarrou is involved in both the narrative
and the action, fighting the plague alongside Rieux and forming a
close alliance of companionship with him. This means that among
Camus's protagonists he is almost unique in combining intellect and
engagement. The existential gap between the physical world and
our powers of reasoning frequently results in existential characters
who either think or do. Tarrou crosses the borderline, not just providing quirky, eccentric accounts of the effects of the plague, not
just working tirelessly alongside Rieux, but critically sustaining a
theory of the plague that motivates his actions.

This theory contains elements familiar to readers of Camus by
now. Tarrou undergoes a traumatic event that forces him to recognise he is not innocent but guilty. And this trauma occurs when he
sees his father, a lawyer, condemn a man to death. The shocking juxtaposition of his father's calm if emphatic pronouncement and the
excessive violence of taking a man's life, reveals to Tarrou the madness of society and the intrinsic aggression of men that, even if
controlled and organised, cannot be eliminated. Tarrou recognises
that every individual is capable of causing mortal harm to another,
and for this reason we are all contaminated, to some extent, by the
plague. Tarrou uses the term 'plague' here as a metaphor for a kind
of violence that is born from having superiority or dominance over
another. He declares that there are plagues and there are victims; we
can either suffer, or cause the suffering, and there are no alternative
positions to inhabit.

A popular interpretation of *La Peste* is to read it as an allegory of
Nazi activity during the Second World War. There are descriptions
of trains full of dead bodies hurtling towards large incinerators,
reminscent of the concentration camps. There are quarantine areas
with all the misery and dehumanisation of the prisoner of war
camps. Finally the siege mentality of the Oranais, cut off from loved
ones, fearful and confused by the power of the plague, recalls the
Occupation in France. Tarrou's symbolism of the plague as the spirit
that caused the murderous desires underlying the war is readily
apparent in declarations such as: 'Il me semble que l'histoire m'a
donné raison, aujourd'hui c'est à qui tuera le plus. Ils sont tous dans
la fureur de meutre, et ils ne peuvent pas faire autrement' (It seems

that history has proved me right, and today it's all about who can do the most killing. They are all mad with aggression, and they can do nothing about it). This is a persuasive reading, but while the historical specificity of war plays a part in the construction of *La Peste*, such a reading would deny the open ambiguity of the text and its many interpretative possibilities. It is still first and foremost a narrative about the response of a community to the imminent possibility of a terrifying and unjust death from disease. The very link between war and plague demonstrates how similar situations can be created by different conditions.

What is interesting is the way that specific historical suffering reminds us of those essential, pressing questions that we still have not solved, questions that I opened this chapter with such as: what is the meaning of life when we know we have to die, and how can we prevent that death from happening prematurely at the hand of another? In this chapter at least, Tarrou is the last in a long line of protagonists who have been forced into asking such questions and finding only partial, imperfect answers to them. Tarrou shows a fierce desire to isolate himself from the violence of humanity, but recognises how difficult this would be. He is obsessed with learning how one could become a saint, that is to say, someone who performed the miracle of hurting no one. Tarrou's fearless and selfless efforts to save others during the plague, his strength of purpose and his sympathy for Rieux are rewarded only by death.

But of course this death is profoundly ambiguous. He is struck down by the plague as it seems that it has finally been beaten, retreating as unexpectedly as it arrived. Tarrou's death is just as pointless and amoral as the others, and yet, in the way that it seems to ensure the subsequent health of the community, there is more than a touch of saintliness to his demise. But Tarrou cannot be said to have fulfilled his claim to hurt no one. Rieux, who survives and who should, by the rules of epic narrative, be allowed the moral glory of his victorious engagement with the plague, is left to mourn his friend bitterly, knowing that: 'il n'y aura jamais plus de paix possible pour lui-même' (never again will he find peace). *La Peste* sets up a number of pressing questions: is there, or is there not a 'meaning' we can assign to the plague? Can man ever act in complete solidarity with others or does his alienation ultimately prove impossible to overcome? What was the correct response to the plague, and did Rieux's selfless but emotionless attitude exemplify it? The reader is, however, unable to deduce any clear answers. The crisis of the plague, when it comes again, will find us just as unprepared and confused as ever.

In the battle that constitutes life and death, there are no winners. Nor are there any clear rules to guide us, no matter how much we long for certainties and absolutes. The frustration and the challenge facing the reader of existentialist texts is to acknowledge the lucidity and the profundity of their thought while recognising that it helps us not at all with the daily business of existing. As these texts ably testify, there can be no clear ethical guidance that could guarantee our irreproachably moral behaviour, for our actions remain in constant disquieting tension with the reasons we produce to justify them. Equally, while life is full of paradoxes and contradictions there are no solutions, for the many excellent and vital questions we formulate never receive any useful answers. The best we can do is to recognise that we are guilty sinners while never failing to aspire to the status of heroes and saints.

Suggested reading

Eric Mathews, *Twentieth Century French Philosophy* (Oxford: Oxford University Press, 1996). A study of Sartrean existentialism, among other theories (including Merleau-Ponty and phenomenology), that succeeds in remaining lucid and accessible throughout.

Germaine Brée, *Camus and Sartre: Crisis and Commitment* (London: Calder & Boyars, 1972) Comprehensive and clear textual analysis that usefully considers both writers.

Rhiannon Goldthorpe, *Sartre: Literature and Theory* (Cambridge: Cambridge University Press, 1984). Sophisticated study of Sartre's philosophical and fictional work.

Philip Thody, *Jean-Paul Sartre: A Literary and Political Study* (London: Hamish Hamilton, 1960). A critique of Sartre's texts that, despite its date, remains relevant and useful.

Conor Cruise O'Brien, *Camus* (London: Fontana Modern Masters/Collins, 1970). An intelligent, provocative study of Camus's life and works.

James S. Williams, *Camus. La Peste* (London: Grant & Cutler, 2000). An excellent introductory guide to this challenging text.

4

Experiments in Form:

The Art of Losing the Plot

By the end of the 1940s, existentialism and the whole notion of *littérature engagée* was falling out of aesthetic favour. Ready to take its place at the cutting edge of literary endeavour was a new, bold form of experimentalism. There is a belief that sits far more comfortably with French culture than with, for instance, the pragmatic British, that literature can have revolutionary power. Such a belief has its roots in a sophisticated understanding of the relationship between language and the world we live in. If we accept that we have no other means of expressing what we perceive, what we believe, and what we experience apart from language, then language has tremendous power for determining reality. We are completely dependent on language for our interractions with others and for our philosophical and political conceptions of how the world works. Even our own most intimate voice of consciousness speaks to us. So, it follows that, if language is our unique and supreme tool of expression, it is less the case that we come to language and use it as we please, than that language determines us and limits our possibilities for being.

Now, this may seem at first glance to imprison humanity in a depressingly fixed and passive relationship to language, but of course there are a number of ways in which we regularly test and expand the formulations of language, and literature is a prime example. One of literature's main devices is what is known as defamiliarisation, or the art of making the familiar seem strange, different, and new. Consider the way that poetry mangles syntax and displaces words from their usual contexts to create meanings that are elusive and complex but intensely evocative, or the way that literature can shake us out of complacent modes of thinking or highlight the complexities in the most fundamental emotions of love, anger and fear. Literary texts challenge us to confront unpleasant truths, and ask harsh questions about what we take for granted, hence the modern French belief that literature can be revolutionary, or, even more explicitly, that there can be no proper, effective revolution without a fundamental change taking place at the level of language. No society can truly change unless it changes the way that it thinks, and literature offers a kind of laboratory in which old conventions can be analysed and new possibilities dramatised.

In the middle of the twentieth century, literature's propensity to demand a wholesale reappraisal of society, and the experience of being a subject within it, would result in a series of plays and novels that contained an implicit political agenda. Paradoxically they expressed their message in ways that were increasingly intellectual and abstract. This is because they would seek to explore the way that the web of language holds a certain vision of reality in place. These literary works would look in two directions at once; towards an understanding of the way that language provides conventions and regulations that tame and control reality, and, with even more verve and abandon, towards the violence and meaninglessness that language conceals.

These texts would be shocking in the extreme as they would systematically challenge every comfortable and comforting convention on which our understanding of reality was based. They would take as their starting point the absurdity of the human condition, the lack of essence to the self, the absence of meaning in the world, the pointlessness of existence. They would demonstrate, rather than suggest, that all human interaction was little more than the play of language in an endless continuum of space and time. Their most provocative move would be to explore the belief, not that life imitated art, but that artistic structures – in particular the idea of a plot; a beginning, a middle and an end organised by meaningful cause and effect – gave life the only structure and substance it had. In other words, if we accept the determining power of language, then we have to understand that stories, the supreme achievement of language to order and cohere experience, give us only the illusion of mastery over our environment and our bodies within it. Once we have been robbed of this illusion then the disquieting truth of the human condition must be faced. To explore the implications of this truth experimental writers began by dismantling the structures of their own work, removing plots, characters and conclusions, some with aggression, some with manipulative cunning and others with comic despair. Two important literary movements came to prominence in the middle of the century, each exploring through experiments in form the consequences of the power we invest in language. Drama was reinvigorated by the Theatre of the Absurd and narrative form challenged by the *nouveau roman* (new novel).

Le théâtre de l'absurde: making a spectacle of life

Modern theatre's desire to unleash a tidal wave of anarchic energy onto the stage had in fact been gathering momentum since the end of the 1800s. In 1896 a two-night run of Alfred Jarry's shocking farce, *Ubu Roi*, offered a taste of what was to come. A vicious political attack on the ruling classes ridiculing their perceived love of money, desire for power, and limited mentalities, it also experimented with a new kind of stage craft. This highlighted the visual aspects of theatre (notably by way of mime and masks), and it sought to undermine language's power to signify (by using nonsensical dialogue). The emotive impact of Jarry's work, bypassing the intellect and appealing instead to the senses and the imagination, lies at the heart of Antonin Artaud's theory of theatre. In 1932 Artaud outlined his theory for what he termed the *théâtre de la cruauté* (theatre of cruelty), whose cruelty was intended for the audience rather than the actors. The theatre would be cruel in that it would rob the spectators of their belief in themselves as decent, moral folk by dramatising on stage the wild, base instincts of humanity.

In a now famous metaphor, Artaud compares the dynamic rush of revelation in those who witness his theatre to the apocalyptic effects of a plague. Although his descriptions linger vividly on the bodily suffering of plague victims, his intention is more to reach the diseased corners in the minds of his spectators. Diseased for Artaud means dully conventional, deadened by routine thought and behaviour, divorced from the amoral energies of life. His theatre performs an act of purification in the way that it 'dénoue des conflits, il dégage des forces, il déclenche des possibilités, et si ces possibilités et ces forces sont noires, c'est la faute non pas de la peste ou du théâtre, mais de la vie' (unfolds conflicts, it unleashes forces, it opens up possibilities; and if these possibilities and these forces are dark the fault lies not with theatre or the plague, but with life). The idea is that the audience, while watching the dramatic spectacle on stage, should undergo an extreme form of catharsis. Rather than identify with the sufferings and triumphs of the characters on stage, however, the identification would take place on another level altogether; the level of unconscious repression where the individual has tucked away violent and erotic instincts according to the demands of civilised society. The kind of theatre that would put spectators back in touch with their primal selves was, according to Artaud, a highly stylised, visually powerful one that dispensed with traditional dialogue and conventional plot in favour of shocking images of incest, rape, murder (for instance). The only difficulty was that the special effects Artaud's plays demanded – a jet of blood that flies across the stage, live scorpions teeming from a woman's genitals – were so tricky to stage that few of his works were ever actually produced. However, the notion of stripping away the veneer of civilisation, exploding the values of good taste and intellectual significance in order to present the audience with a brutal and disquieting image of their fundamental reality would continue to take the theatre by storm. But it resulted in a form of stagecraft that emphasised its own artificiality in order to reach more profound existential truths.

The playwrights of the *théâtre de l'absurd*, writing and producing their plays at the end of the 1940s and throughout the 50s, shared some common dramatic concerns that they explored in significantly different ways. They were concerned with the reality of the stage – the space and time of the theatrical event, the fact that it was witnessed by a captive audience – and the way its dimensions and rules could be seen to correspond metaphorically to the dimensions and rules of human life. They dispensed with logical, credible plots in favour of static, highly visual, often shocking or distressing situations in order to dramatise a more abstract truth of the human condition. And without exception they all, one way or another, gave the audience a hard time.

One of the fiercest attacks undertaken by dramatists was on the traditional belief that the human condition has meaning. Samuel Beckett, in arguably the most famous work of absurdist drama, *En Attendant Godot* (Waiting for Godot), presents us with the plight of two tramps, Vladimir and Estragon, stranded in an interminable wait for the mysterious and stubbornly absent Godot. The stage set is empty apart from a single tree. A uniform grey light undermines the distinction between night and day. There is no explanation for the state the protagonists find themselves in, and there will ultimately be no release from it. Nothing distracts us from the process of waiting itself and the tramps' obsession with passing the time. Sounds difficult to watch? On its first performance in Paris, when the curtains opened on the second act to reveal the unchanged set (to be fair, the tree now has a few leaves) most of the audience who had not left in the intermission felt they could bear it no longer and walked out. Yet the relentless lack of dramatic interest (in the conventional sense) allows for a subtle, tragicomic exploration of human interaction.

Vladimir and Estragon have a certain amount of time and space to fill; that is their theatrical project as well, in a broader sense, as their existential condition as men. The play passes in a stream of dialogue that is often surreal, occasionally nonsensical, but always tuned in to the dynamic rhythms of human relationships. They bicker and repel each other, seek mutual comfort and attempt moments of tenderness. They appeal to a latent sense of their individual autonomy but quickly fall back into the security of mutual dependence. When they consider hanging themselves from a rope in the tree (an act of ambivalent motivation drawing on frustration and despair but also on their curiosity in trying out something new) they decide against it for the reason that one might be left alone. Beckett is quick to alert us to the absurd origins of their relationship, pointing out that the foundation of their togetherness is not instinctual attraction but the bleak necessity of sharing a stage. But that arbitrary bond is immediately invested with troubled emotions: when Estragon shouts: 'Ne me touche pas! Ne me demande rien! Ne me dis rien! Reste avec moi!' (Don't touch me! Don't question me! Don't speak to me! Stay with me!), he expresses both the unbearable irritation of Vladimir's presence and his overriding fear of being alone. Bleak as the situation is for Beckett's tramps, it could be worse; they might not have each other, they might not have Godot. Feeble as these defences are, they nevertheless shield them from the unacceptable horror that is the radical emptiness at the heart of the human condition.

Yet while this emptiness is continually evoked, it is always evaded:

'On trouve toujours quelque chose, hein, Didi, pour nous donner l'impression d'exister? (Estragon: We always find something, eh Didi, to give us the impression we exist?) by the tramps' cunning and often comical role-play, their relentless word-play, the shreds of vaudeville, circus and farce provided by their interactions with Lucky and Pozzo, characters whose master-slave dynamic offers a contrast to Vladimir and Estragon's uneasy companionship. In denuding his characters of quotidian attributes and refusing them any justification for their presence on stage, Beckett emphasises instead a kind of common, base humanity that links his actors to the hapless, trapped audience. Dispossessed tramps transform symbolically, alarmingly, into figures of everyman. We see them struggling to transcend their lumpen anonymity, trying to deny the futility of existence, longing for meaning and purpose, and failing, again and again, to find them. The constructed nature of human identity is further emphasised by the structural similarities between actors and spectators. Theatrical role-play, the creation of a character that exists only in and through the process of speaking a rag-bag of selected dialogue, performance after performance, offers an eerie echo of identity creation beyond the stage. The brief temporality of the theatrical experience, a burst of dramatic interest on an otherwise dark and empty stage seems uncomfortably close to Pozzo's despairing description of life: 'Elles accouchent à cheval sur une tombe, le jour brille un instant, puis c'est la nuit à nouveau' (They give birth astride a grave, daylight gleams for a moment, and then night falls again). Theatre to slit your wrists to, if it weren't for the unaccountable but undeniable comedy that informs and lightens every barren interaction.

Beckett can seem quite kindly and avuncular when compared to the nihilistic ravings of Eugène Ionesco. Ionesco's plays also combine black comedy and the dramatic expression of fear in the face of the human condition. But whereas Beckett's plays steadfastly refuse to stage an event, Ionesco's offer a pyrotechnical display of wild and explosive violence. The key to understanding Ionesco's work is to recognise that it dramatises the parallel universe of the nightmare, where surreal or impossible events produce a genuinely fearful response from the dreamer. Like nightmares, Ionesco's plays have no plot line as such. Instead they stage the breakdown of a bizarre but not necessarily threatening situation into total chaos and disorder. For instance in *La Leçon* (The Lesson) the teacher's relationship to the student becomes increasingly violent and aggressive as the student fails to repeat the word 'couteau' (knife) to the teacher's satisfaction. The frenzy of their dialogue reaches fever pitch as the teacher stabs the student with a knife that Ionesco suggests could be imaginary, in order to highlight the way the word itself becomes a weapon. The professor is then chastised by his servant who scolds him and slaps him until he reaches a state of servile obedience, at which point another student arrives. This brief outline does no justice to the eccentric, punning force of the dialogue, or to the emotional charge of the characters' interaction, or to the way that events follow a kind of illogical but necessary causal chain. As characters slide from one crazy scenario to another and the sense of tension and panic accelerates, there is an inevitability to the play's progression that takes the place of rational motivation. The loss of control that characterises Ionesco's plays taps into a deep-seated human fear that the structures of reason and sense that rein in life's chaotic underside are simply too fragile for the task.

One of those fundamental structures, language, is under vicious attack. Exchanges between characters are never less than bizarre, but frequently language fragments and dissolves into meaningless phonic sounds. In *La Cantatrice chauve* (The Bald Primadonna) the two couples, the Martins and the Smiths, named after characters in Ionesco's English grammar books, speak in banal and stilted phrases reminiscent of early language learners (this tends to strike a chord with most foreign language students), until these phrases, which never respond to one another, melt into a stream of unrelated words:

> Mme. Martin: Bazar, Balzac, Bazaine!
> M. Martin: Bizarre, beaux-arts, baisers!
> M. Smith: A, c, I, o, u, a, c, I, o, u, a, c, I, o, u, I!
> Mme. Martin: B, c, d, f, g, l, m, n, p, r, s, t, v, w, x, z!

This seems impossible to approach analytically, and indeed it is, for at no point does Ionesco ask us to apply reason to the madness of his stagecraft. Instead the breakdown of language is an event that spectators are forced to participate in, as they are assaulted by the extravagant energy of Ionesco's dramas. Once its referential function is lost, language becomes pure energy, channelled into the guttural shouts and cries of the characters. There is no sense of mismatch between dialogue and characters as characters are stereotypic and robotic, lacking individuation, divorced from human sentiment except for a genuine fear of the events occurring on stage. The real scene stealers in Ionesco's plays are the objects which have a far greater presence and reality than the puppet-like actors. In *Les Chaises* (The Chairs), where an elderly couple prepare the stage for the arrival of a great orator (who of course, when he finally appears, cannot speak), Ionesco demands that the chairs accumulate at great speed, filling the stage with their 'absences présentes' (empty presences) until finally: 'les chaises ne représentent plus les personnages déterminés [...] mais bien la foule. Elles jouent toutes seules' (the chairs no longer represent specific characters, but instead the crowd itself. They are acting on their own). Similarly, in *L'Avenir est dans les oeufs* (The Future is in Eggs), eggs accumulate until the stage itself collapses. In Ionesco's dramatic world there is a threatening superabundance of objects, an avalanche of materiality whose brute power of being is superior to that of frail humanity, not least because it is entirely without emotion. This cumulative force of objects, married to the inhumanity of the characters and the fragmentation of language, produces what can be termed a 'happening', a dramatic event whose intensity provokes a visceral, or bodily, response in its spectators. The elements of Ionesco's stage craft would seem to repel and resist critical study but students tend to love the rebellious spirit of the plays, and their crazy, potent anarchy.

If we are to talk of happenings and spectacles, the greatest stage magician of them all is Jean Genet, the bad boy of modern French literature. Genet's plays perform a critique of traditional power relations whereby one group (white, indigenous, heterosexual, male) is given unfair and unnatural dominance over its opposite (black, immigrant, gay, female). Genet's mission is by no means to provoke the kind of social outcry that would result in practical help for the oppressed, although this does not mean his plays are not political. Genet's eccentric desire is first and foremost to glorify and celebrate the baseness and degradation of such socially reviled identities, essentially because he, as a homosexual thief, feels himself to be one of them. In 'Comment jouer *Les Bonnes*' (How *Les Bonnes* should be acted) he declares: 'Je vais au théâtre afin de me voir sur la scène [...] tel que je ne saurais – ou n'oserais – me voir ou me rêver, et tel pourtant, que je me sais être' (I go to the theatre in order to see myself on the stage [..] in a way that I wouldn't know how – or wouldn't dare – to see or fantasise, and yet in a way that I know myself to be). Genet's concern here, beyond glorifying the heroism of the oppressed, is to recognise that calling someone gay or a thief is to put them in a kind of straitjacket of identity that allows no room for individuality and difference. Unlike Beckett's characters who are searching though role-play to put an identity together, Genet's characters have ready-made identities imposed upon them. Hence his plays show these characters in a state of angry and aggressive rebellion, conscious of the despised role they have been forced to occupy, collaborating despite themselves in their oppression, and frustratingly aware that their authenticity is elsewhere and unimaginable.

In *Les Bonnes* (The Maids), the two maids, Claire and Solange, play with their state of submission to their thoughtlessly affectionate employer, Madame, by acting out a series of private fantasies. When the curtains first open, the audience watches a scene between Madame and one of her maids where the dialogue is intimate, stagy, shot through with undercurrents of condescension, aggression and eroticism. Then an alarm clock rings and the maids return to their usual roles, leaving the startled spectators to realise they have been witnessing a role-play fantasy. Genet here demonstrates the inherent theatricality of identity, the way that it is only a question of convincing acting. Undermining the borderline between acting and being, between fantasy and reality, is a significant element of Genet's plays. *Le Balcon* (The Balcony) is staged in a brothel where the customers dress up as figures of power (judges, bishops etc) and once in costume 'become' them, degrading and idolising them simultaneously, for those who are oppressed long both to become and to destroy their so-called masters.

We can witness these contradictory emotions in *Les Bonnes* where Solange declares to 'Madame' played by Claire: 'Je vous hais! Je hais votre poitrine pleine de souffles embaumés. Votre poitrine ... d'ivoire! Vos cuisses ... d'or! Vos pieds ... d'ambre! (Elle crache sur la robe rouge.) Je vous hais!' (I hate you! I hate your breast that heaves with fragrant sighs. Your breast ... of ivory! Your thighs ... of gold! Your feet ... of amber! (She spits on the red dress) I hate you!). Yet the mixture of eroticism and hatred topples over into murderous aggression as the maids plot to poison Madame's tea. When Madame fails to drink the tea they have prepared, the maids swiftly resume their role play and see it through to its natural conclusion. Claire (as Madame) assumes her role of authority over Solange and, against Solange's desires, drinks the poison. This is again a dramatic situation that cannot be understood through logical reasoning, but which finds its motivation in the dark, paradoxical corners of the unconscious mind. In a play about the power of fantasy and the seductive fascination of the image, the triumph of fantasy seems appropriate.

Genet's plays, then, focus on the way that the structures of power, identity and sexuality (structures entirely responsible for assigning us our places in society) find their origins not in material reality but in the uncertain and cloudy realms of fantasy and illusion. Genet highlights the artificiality of what we take for granted by keeping his plays resolutely non-realistic. Genet demands that his actors act as if they were acting, and in fact suggested that the maids could be played by men. Not only does this keep the necessary distance between actor and role, but it insists further on the performative nature of any identity, even gender identity. The example of the maid's discourse quoted above is clearly not the way a 'real' maid would talk, and in *Les Nègres* (The Blacks) the difference between black and white is extravagantly highlighted by the use of make-up, masks and some wincingly vulgar costumes. Genet requires such glaring artifice in order to attack the notion of identity as being somehow 'natural', particularly when the identities in question – master/slave, black/white – are charged with cultural values. Identity is all a matter of representation for Genet; it is always an acting out of a pre-ordained image, hence the unspeakable injustice of designating certain identities as culturally less valid. Archibald declares in *Les Nègres*: 'Que les nègres se nègrent. Qu'ils s'obstinent jusqu'à la folie dans ce qu'on les condamne à être' (May the blacks become blacker. May they insist to the point of madness on acting out the identity to which they are condemned) meaning that the only 'choice' the blacks have is not to accept passively the identity they have had imposed on them, but to act it out in an extreme form of parody.

The main force of Genet's vitriol is reserved for a culture that manipulates its subjects into dichotomies of white and black, organised on faultlines of power. His plays explore through ritual and role-play the processes by which those manipulative cultural images are formed, subverted, but ultimately reinforced. Often, however, Genet's attack is directed towards the audience. *Les Nègres* demands a white audience to insult, or failing that, a life-sized white doll placed on the front row towards which the hatred of unthinking white superiority could be directed. Such a move demonstrates symbolically the way that Genet, and theatre of the absurd as a whole, views its audiences as misguided, unenlightened, culturally stupefied individuals who need to be shocked from their complacency into accepting the tormented, but philosophically sophisticated, view of the world espoused by the absurdists. Audiences are forced into uncomfortably voyeuristic positions by Genet, disquieted by tedium and repetition in Beckett, and set upon by the aggressive panic of chaos in Ionesco's plays, all in the cause of a more authentic understanding of the bleak nature of reality.

The *nouveau roman*: art as reality

At the same time as spectators were being challenged by experimental theatre, readers were also being forced into new forms of engagement with literary texts. The term 'nouveau roman' was applied to the works of a number of writers (among them Alain Robbe-Grillet, Michel Butor, Claude Simon and Nathalie Sarraute) who were keen to expose traditional realism as a set of artificial conventions. 'Realism' designates the style employed in texts that describe the world in a way that is instantly recognisable to the reader. If the hero of a novel is described as 'tall, dark and handsome', we immediately know the type of man our imagination should conjure up, and we have a pretty good idea of the role he will play in the story. In actual fact the adjectives 'tall, dark and handsome' are imprecise words to describe someone and could cover a wide range of very different individuals. But for most novels this is irrelevant; such descriptions are short-cuts, appealing to codes and conventions that structure narratives in all media – texts, films, television – and which find their origins, not in reality (given the disappointing scarcity of tall, dark, handsome men), but in fiction in any case.

However, once we really start to explore narrative conventions, not least the way that plot puts a framework of organisation on top of otherwise random events, we can see just how seductive and insidious such supposed artifice may be. Stories are satisfying because they give us the comfort of meaning; a sense that, no matter how tragic or irrational or unexpected an event, it has a place in the scheme of cause and effect that lead to the narrative's ending. The sense of causality is rooted deep in the human psyche. As children, we learn the sophisticated processes of explanation and justification, and as we grow older, memory organises experience in retrospect, so that even recalcitrant experiences like being ill or falling in love are shored up by webs of reasoning. Stories are not simply an extension of this process, but rather the perfect templates of organisation against which we judge reality. Stories tell us how things ought to be, and reality is often a rather shambolic and unsatisfactory approximation of their smooth perfection. One of the main aims of the *nouveau roman* is to expose the well-oiled machinery of narrative for what it is. Rather than relating stories as if they were innocent transpositions of everyday events, self-reflexive narrative alerts readers to the process of writing as it organises and even determines our understanding of reality.

One of the advantages narrative has over reality is the prospect of an imminent conclusion. Endings are paramount in stories; they tell us who was right or wrong, who was good or bad, they resolve problems and find solutions to seemingly impossible situations. Narrative thrives on conflict, so most novels can be boiled down to simple formulations. Something is lost, a problem is posed, and the narrative works to restore order and harmony. The detective story is a perfect example of a wild event that is tamed and controlled by narrative. A violent murder represents a tear in the fabric of our knowledge. It is itself the end of a story of jealousy, greed or hatred, but a story that has passed by unnoticed and needs to be reconstructed, piece by piece. Generally detective novels toy with the reader, offering them fragments of knowledge that cannot be cohered into a structure, but which promise enlightenment when the climax of the narrative is reached. This is why literary theorists talk about narrative as delayed truth. Truth is revealed at the end, that is the pact that narrative makes with its readers, and reading is the pleasurably frustrating business of waiting for that truth to arrive.

In Robbe-Grillet's version of the detective novel, *Les Gommes* (The Rubbers), these age-old certainties are treated to a radical reappraisal. In the first place, there has been no murder. The bullet misses its intended victim, the academic Dupont, who, for his own reasons, chooses to go into hiding. He thus leaves the detective, Wallas, to follow up clues and hypotheses that will clearly not cohere. Wallas does not inspire our confidence. Usually the presence of the detective is the guarantor of truth; the detective is powerful because he is a better reader than anyone else. His interpretations of events and his ability to imagine causal links make him the obvious person to re-establish order. But Wallas is not on form; he is tired and unable to think clearly, he has a poor track record of imposing meaning: 'Autrefois il lui est arrivé trop souvent de se laisser prendre aux cercles du doute et de l'impuissance' (In the past he let himself be trapped all too frequently in circles of doubt and impotence). Worst of all, he cannot hypothesise successfully. His meetings with Laurent, the chief of police, are unsatisfactory because he cannot convince this sceptic of the truth of his suppositions: 'les paroles les plus simples prennent, dans sa bouche, un aspect equivoque' (the simplest phrases, coming from his mouth, take on an equivocal air).

Of course this is why Wallas fails as a detective. He cannot impose meaning because he cannot manipulate language to create the appearance of reality. With Wallas unable to take control of his investigation, mysteries multiply in the text, and Wallas himself loses the plot in more ways than one. Just as his continual perambulations around the town repeatedly fail to take him to its centre, forcing him back to the aptly named Boulevard Circulaire (Ring Road), so Wallas's own journey through the mystery takes him on a circuitous route to the scene of the crime. Only this time it is Wallas, with the revolver in his hand, who is startled into shooting the unfortunate Dupont. How are we to understand the causality of a text that transforms the detective into the murderer? The delayed crime is empty of meaning (just as the town is missing its centre) and Wallas's investigations have resolved nothing, only produced infinite complications.

To think of this text as a text without structure would be a mistake. In fact it is a highly structured, cunningly manipulative text that plays with all the rules of the detective genre. Wallas's watch stops when the first attempt is made on Dupont's life, and the shock of the revolver firing sets if off again at precisely 7.30 the following evening. The 24 hours of Wallas's enquiry, which make up the time of the narrative, become a kind of insertion into the fabric of time, or rather a time outside of time, which is, after all, the temporality in which any narrative functions. Narrative is an arena in which anything can happen, if language wills it so, and here the narrative makes up for its earlier faults in failing to commit a crime, by replacing the murderer with Wallas. To do so it breaks one cast-iron rule of sense creation: it fails to respect the difference between a detective and a murderer, collapsing these two necessarily separate roles onto the one figure.

So Robbe-Grillet confounds our expectations by forcing the reader to analyse what those expectations were in the first place. And then he shows us that those expectations are purely conventions that are not essential but constructed. In another of his texts, *La Jalousie*, the issue of interpretation is highlighted. The title itself can mean either 'jealousy' or 'venetian blind' and this split echoes the ambivalence of the text that could either be organised through the narrating voice of a man who does not reveal his identity, or through the impassive lens of a camera, recording what it sees with perfect objectivity. Once we lack the personalised voice of a narrator telling us his story, we realise to what extent we depend upon such a voice to anchor our reading. Set on a banana plantation in an unspecified tropical country, the narrative repeats obsessively certain scenes between A (the presumed narrator's wife) and Franck (the wife's presumed lover) which may or may not prove his wife's infidelity. When A gets out of Franck's car, does she lean over to kiss him, or to pick up a parcel? When they are forced to stay overnight in the town, are their reasons innocent or guilty ones? The repetition of such scenes is difficult to account for unless a jealous husband is replaying over and over in his mind the grounds he has for his suspicions. But because we as readers have no context for these scenes, and no other, external viewpoint on the characters, we cannot solve the mystery.

Instead we are forced to concentrate upon the way in which these (non)events are represented. The reader then becomes increasingly aware that jealousy inhabits the viewing perspective, distorting and colouring its descriptions. Jealousy accounts for what could then be read as hallucinations and painful fantasies, caused by the torments of a troubled mind. But if we accept the presence of the jealous husband, then we have to accept that the descriptions which we initially read as wholly objective have now turned out to be profoundly subjective. The random disorder of the narrative's structure is in fact a precise account of a psychological state of mind. The problems the (supposed) narrator encounters in interpreting A's behaviour, the 'is she?' or 'isn't she?' of A's infidelities, are mirrored by the difficulties the reader has in working out what is going on. But as we ask ourselves, is there or isn't there a narrator?, so the processes of readerly interpretation are highlighted. Readers catch themselves out as they search for the faintest traces of the structures that usually guide their progress through a narrative, or dig out the clues embedded in the text that might allow them the luxury of one certainty on which an interpretation could be founded.

While this is a narrative about readers reading, it is also a story that demonstrates how writing is always already a reading. Narrative is always motivated by a desire that exceeds the simple desire to recount; a subtext of complex emotions inhabits the most seemingly innocent of descriptions. Robbe-Grillet cleverly shows us how even descriptions which could be objective recordings from a camera could equally well be the jealous ravings of an obsessive. In other words, language is never pure. It is always creating an argument, subtly, implicitly. It is impossible to prevent language from telling a story, impossible to empty it completely of opinion or perspective. There is a famous image in *La Jalousie* of a flawed pane of glass that distorts the landscape beyond the window. The implication is that language is a similar medium, a supposedly transparent window on external reality whose internal flaws and quirks can make things appear and disappear depending on the perspective taken. Yet if Robbe-Grillet would work to undermine the magic of narrative by explaining away its tricks, he succeeds only in extending and intensifying the power of narrative to organise and control every aspect of our relation with reality.

The *nouveau roman*, then, is fascinated by the organisational power of narrative, but as it explores this power, it also creates

new forms of narrative, new ways of representing reality. Within
the group as a whole, there is a constant preoccupation with the
limits of our perception and the way those limits are defined by
language. While *nouveaux romanciers* like Alain Robbe-Grillet play
with the structures and the conventions that determine our
understanding of the world, other new novelists, like Nathalie
Sarraute, are concerned with expanding the horizons of our perception. Sarraute attempts to open up a new relationship between
language and the body through her representation of tropisms.
The term 'tropism' is borrowed from the natural sciences where
it indicates movements of response to external stimuli such as
heat or light. Sarraute draws the reader's attention to the level of
instinctual responses that underlie human behaviour, suggesting
they are too rapid and removed from consciousness to be readily
apparent to perception. What she is referring to is the level of
experience that seems barely human; instinctual reflexes of
aggression and recoil, fear and desire that motivate the more controlled responses of speech and gesture. To represent these
tropistic reactions, time is oddly warped within her texts and language is set free from its realistic constraints to become figurative
and metaphoric. Reading a novel by Sarraute is to dispense with
plot entirely and to consider a series of – usually quotidian –
scenes through a slow-motion, magnifying camera. A Sarrautian
moment can expand over several pages of narration and incorpo-
rate numerous reflexes of anger, hatred, vulnerability, insecurity
and longing. Take, for example, this passage from *Le Planétarium*
(The Planetarium) in which the only action involved is that of a
man dialling a telephone number:

'C'est le premier mouvement qu'il fait vers la délivrance; c'est
un défi qu'il leur lance, à eux tous là-bas, de cette étroite
cabine au fond du petit bistrot, en composant ce numéro: un
simple numéro de téléphone comme les autres en apparence,
et cette apparance banale a quelque chose d'émouvant, elle
rehausse son caractère magique: c'est le talisman qu'il porte
toujours sur lui – sa sauvegarde quand il sent menacé. C'est le
mot de passe révélé aux rares privilégiés […] Il se sent comme
un homme traqué sur un sol étranger, qui sonne à la porte de

l'ambassade d'un pays civilisé, puissant, de son pays, pour
demander asile...'

(This is the first step he takes towards deliverance; a gesture of
defiance he throws at them all down there, from this narrow
booth at the back of the little bistro, by dialling this number. A
simple telephone number, just like any other in appearance,
and the very banality of its appearance moves him somehow, it
heightens its magical character: it's the talisman he always carries with him, his safeguard for when he feels threatened. It's
the password revealed to a privileged few [...] He feels like a
hunted man on foreign soil, who rings the doorbell of the
embassy of a country that is civilised, powerful, familiar, in
order to seek asylum...)

The narration does not take us through the action of telephoning
someone, but through the minutiae of psychic motivations and
emotional responses for doing so. Note too the language of the passage which alerts the reader to changes in the emotional climate by
means of metaphors drawn from other fictional discourses:
délivrance, talisman, mot de passe, demander asile. We are swiftly alerted
to the religious and mystical connotations of the narrator's actions,
as well as a sense of escape more appropriate to the spy novel.
Sarraute uses vocabulary that is heavily charged with drama and passion so that it functions appropriately on the reader's responses,
despite being transplanted to an unusual context. The reader can
then keep up with the swift changes in mental landscape that constitute what stands for plot in these novels. The action in Sarraute's
texts is always elsewhere to the action and it is always the same: a
continual subterranean war between her characters, who each seek
to impose an ideal image of their identity on others and hide or disguise their own tropistic reactions. Identity for Sarraute is always
fluid, dynamic and unstable, despite the character's best efforts to
project controlled and valid images of themselves. Not only do they
have to fight the destabilising force of tropistic reactions but they
must also withstand the penetrating and malevolent gaze of others,
who almost always seek to undermine their integrity.

In Sarraute's evocative metaphors, the other is represented as vindictive, appropriative, demanding, or unkind, as a leech or vampire or parasite. Appropriately for a narrative that seeks to depict the bodily zone of mental response, the linguistic images are drawn from vulnerable physicality. The shell of the self is often subject to cracking or crumbling, or else like septic skin it fills with pus. Behind this insufficient outer layer, the self of tropistic reactions cowers, trembles, fears the attacks to which it must submit. Violence and aggression are part of our every word and gesture in Sarraute's textual universe, as we are continually and endlessly in conflict with the other. Her narratives are generally structured as a stream of consciousness, tapped into by a number of circulating, fluctuating psyches, running through an endless, seething mass of tropistic reactions. This is why it is misleading to talk about 'characters' in Sarraute's texts. The tropism marks a consciousness that is (re)creating and (re)defining its identity with every word it speaks and every reaction it undergoes. Every single act, word and gesture puts the self in play, places the self at the mercy of others, and marks the arena of a battle in a never-ending war of self-creation and self-survival.

Sarraute's world view rests on a particular belief in the power of language. In Sarraute's texts words are more substantial than the world they seek to represent. Language is performative – that is to say it makes things happen, it gives substance and reality to what would otherwise remain formless and uncertain. It offers us the only grasp on reality that it is possible to have. Furthermore, the level of reality represented by the tropism is only brought into being by Sarraute's narratives. There is no objective way to witness and record these tropistic movements, and so her triumph here is to persuade us of the reality of a world for which there is no actual referent. Language creates the level of consciousness that is the tropistic response as it narrates it. We can see how language effortlessly transcends the boundary between fantasy and reality, failing to mark any particular distinction between the two. In the above quote the smallest action in the 'real' world is the basis for a disproportionate fantasy concerning exile and inclusion, and both real and imaginary, action and metaphor, are essential in constituting the lived identity of the character who speaks. These movements of fantasy provide the very process by which her characters take up a position of identity. Sarraute suggests there can be no identity outside language, and that the language of fiction (of fantasy, of story-telling, of active creation) is also the language of subjectivity.

At the beginning of this chapter I argued that, despite its abstract nature, the work of experimental writers was political, and indeed these authors are political in the sense that they refute a vision of the world that seems to come from a lost era. Rather than see man as the centre of the universe and his powers of reason as the tool with which he masters his world, these texts insist on the anonymity of the individual, the absurdity and resistance of the world that surrounds him, and the dynamic flux of experience. However, the link between language and a psychoanalytic view of identity would subsequently be put to more overtly political use with the events of May 68 demanding that the old heirarchies of power be overturned. One of the most pertinent examples of this is the rise of feminism.

Suggested reading

David Bradby, *Modern French Drama 1940-1980* (Cambridge: Cambridge University Press, 1984). Extensive analysis of a wide range of dramatists, including the absurdists mentioned above. Elegant and interesting readings.

Jacques Guicharnaud, *Modern French Theatre: From Giraudoux to Genet* (New Haven & London: Yale University Press, 1975). Accessible and compelling chapters on Genet, Beckett and Ionesco that deal in detail with a range of their plays.

Peter Norrish, *New Tragedy and Comedy in France, 1945-70* (London: Macmillan Press, 1988). An interesting perspective on theatre of the absurd, as well as other modern French playwrights.

Ann Jefferson, *The Nouveau Roman and the Poetics of Fiction* (Cambridge: Cambridge University Press, 1980). Interprets a range of texts by Robbe-Grillet, Sarraute and Butor with tremendous clarity and insight.

Celia Britton, *The Nouveau Roman: Fiction, Theory and Politics* (Basingstoke & New York: Macmillan, 1992). Useful and engaging on the history and politics of the movement, as well as containing perceptive readings of the texts.

Valerie Minogue, *Nathalie Sarraute and the War of the Words* (Edinburgh: Edinburgh University Press, 1981). A sophisticated, in-depth study of five of Sarraute's novels, including *Le Planétarium*.

5

Women's Writing:

Imagination in Power

In 1949 Simone de Beauvoir wrote the now famous words: 'On ne naît pas femme, on le devient' (One is not born a woman, but becomes one). It is difficult from our contemporary perspective to imagine the incredulity and outrage that such a statement produced. For Beauvoir to suggest that women were not innately maternal, devout, obedient and nurturing but as keen as men for education, power and recognition, was not just political dynamite but also a kind of cultural heresy. Women, or at least the concept of Woman, had long since held a special and particular place in the national imagination. Misogyny was not the issue here, rather a more insidiously crippling glorification of woman as mother and as object of male desire. Identified with the nation itself in the feminine gender of *la* France, *la* République, women were offered protection, adoration and admiration, but at the cost of their personal liberty. Until 1965, a married woman legally required the permission of her husband to practise a profession or open a bank account, and until 1974 abortion was illegal. In gaining basic rights as citizens, French women were notoriously slow off the mark, but they had imposing cultural barriers to overcome, not least an ideal of womanhood that was allied to national interests. In failing to fulfil their assigned roles, women let down a nation that desperately needed to increase the birth-rate, lower the rate of unemployment, and boost the morale of men traumatised by two damaging world wars. Little wonder, then, that Beauvoir's *Le Deuxième Sexe* (The Second Sex) was published in a climate both hostile and resistant to such radical change.

Yet the ideas in Beauvoir's polemical text were to provide the foundations of contemporary French feminist thought and to influence feminists across the globe. Beauvoir argues that women suffer the biological disadvantage of being the sex that bears children. In consequence women have been sidelined economically and culturally, defined only and always as men's 'Other' and reduced to the status of the 'second sex'. Women are thus denied a specific gender identity and defined instead as the opposite of men: weak, passive, romantic, nature's helpmates, homemakers and nurses. Clearly this description of woman's identity fails to touch reality for many, who would be offended (at best) by being denied the possibilities of strength and enterprise. This unacceptable definition provided a springboard for a feminist attack on a simplistic patriarchal vision of women. The subsequent difficulty for feminism was to resist the urge to substitute a supposedly more 'true' set of adjectives in place of the ones it disliked. If patriarchy had refused to see that each woman is unique, feminists could hardly make the same mistake.

The question of women's specificity remains central to all feminist agendas but it has proved notably divisive in French feminist thought. Contemporary French feminism flourished in the period of cultural upheaval that followed the riots of May 1968, a period when all cultural hierarchies of power and systems of repression were violently challenged. Although this was a revolution fought by men and dominated by male agendas, the questions raised resonated in the female student population. Women began to wonder just how the demands for liberation from oppression would involve them, and just how many of their voices would be heard in a newly democratic society. The MLF (Movement de Libération des Femmes), founded in 1970, developed two main agendas: a demand that women regain control over their bodies with the right for both contraception and safe abortions, and a wide-ranging challenge to the prevalent representation of women. Women's image, their desires and their relation to language were reconsidered with the aim of finding more authentic ways of expressing the reality of the female condition. Such common cause was quickly fractured by an antagonistic split between those who argued for equality and those who wished to celebrate – but also isolate – women's specific difference. A small but well-publicised element of the movement chose to boycott the political arena altogether, claiming that it was too hopelessly patriarchal. While such genuine but perhaps excessive attempts to create a pure space for women seem self-defeating, the issue of difference remains highly significant. Clearly there are biological and historical conditions imposed on women, with the result that women often need or desire to conform to a certain stereotype. Yet the fact remains that each woman is individual and unique, different in many ways from that stereotype. The solution is perhaps not to see these two forms of identity – the socially constructed feminine and the repressed and denied feminine – as mutually exclusive, but as existing in a fascinating if complex relationship. In an exploration of such a split female identity, torn between social demands for conformity and an irrepressible urge for self-expression, literature, and particularly writing by women, offers a rich and diverse field of enquiry.

Certainly a concern with women's identity was a notable preoccupation in women's writing in the twentieth century. On the one hand this concern has a political implication; speaking the truth of women's experience is a way of giving voice to a story that has all too often been silenced. On the other hand the concern is metaphysical; identity as it is formed, deformed and reformed, identity in crisis or in the process of transformation, identity as fluid and flexible, or as unstable and fragmented, presents both problems and possibilities in the narratives of some of the best known modern French women writers. Equally prevalent has been a concern with textual innovation and experimentation, with breaking down the boundaries between fact and fiction, autobiography and narrative, fantasy and reality. This is not to say that all women writers are interested in breaking down coherent stereotypical identities and challenging textual conventions, or that those who were interested always acted out of a feminist allegiance. It does suggest that women, occupying a historically marginal role in society, were more able to question and subvert some of its dearly held beliefs, of which our understanding of identity is one. And women, existing in a different relation to power, forced to confine their influence to the erotic and domestic domains, therefore had a different take on power and its organisation, be that within the nucleus of a family or the arena of the literary text. And, finally, if Beauvoir were right, if being a woman *is* an uncomfortable process of becoming that may never achieve its goal, women therefore have a different attitude to identity and gender, alerted to the fragility of its construction and its very lack of inevitability.

Questions of identity and experimentation in language provide the focal points for the readings which I will be undertaking in this chapter. As in the previous chapter, experimentation seeks to undermine conventions that structure reality, but in this instance language is understood as privileging the male conception of reality, and there is a clear political goal in seeking alternatives. I shall explore the way conventions are broken down to make way for originality and innovation in the search for an authentic feminine vision of the world.

Gender identity and sexuality: Colette

The start of the century saw Colette shoot to fame with her 'Claudine' novels, a series of four novels charting the development of Claudine from her schooldays in the provinces to her young married life in Paris. They were racy reads, spiced with lesbian antics, and they became bestsellers. Colette's success was undoubtedly due in part to her then husband, Henri Gaultiers-Villars, known by his pen name, Willy. He ran a publishing factory, putting his name to works written by authors he had commissioned, and the Claudine novels began life in this way. Willy's real genius lay in his ability to market the works he published, and having asked his young wife to write the lightly-disguised and titillating story of her adolescence, he then made the most of the link between Colette and Claudine while never entirely conflating the two. He intended to tease his readership in more ways than one, manipulating their desire to attribute the sexual goings-on to the real persona of Colette, but refusing them the satisfaction of certainty.

The issue at stake here is not just clever publicity, but the realisation that readers long – fallaciously and impossibly – for art and reality to merge. Colette would soon break free from Willy's influence and go on to write more sophisticated and crafted novels than these early potboilers. But in almost all of them her unconventional life would spill over into her texts, resulting in fiction that was covertly autobiographical and autobiographies that were decidedly fictional. On the one hand Colette continued Willy's game of slyly mocking the reader's desire to know the narrator of a text, but on the other she was questioning the very identity of the woman who writes. For Colette, as for many other women writers of the century, her writing persona was distinct and unique, but it was also an intimate part of her personality, just as the stories told were inspired by experience but equally transformed by the demands of narrative. Women writers in the twentieth century would frequently use their subjectivity and their life as a basis for their writing, but, with their desire for experimentation and taste for ambiguity, the end result often challenged all previous conceptions of the link between identity and narrative.

One of Colette's major themes in her stories is the exploration of gender and sexuality and the way that they are formed in the individual. We find in her texts an intuitive awareness of the difficulties women face and a skilful subversion of society's rules and codes. Colette's women are often bound by social convention, but they do their best to make it work for them. In Colette's sexual politics, stereotypical gender roles are frequently subverted. It is a common feature of her work that men are represented primarily as objects of desire, appreciated as lovers, and indulged like children. Male beauty for Colette resides in the attributes of fragility, vulnerability and grace more often associated with the feminine aesthetic, and men are often weak in both their mental and physical constitution. By contrast Colette's women are practical, often cunning, survivors. They rejoice in a kind of streetwise common sense that makes them resilient, strong and perceptive. Yet while these representations may seem radical, Colette nevertheless bows to the conventions of her society. For all their abilities women still inhabit an archetypal feminine world of boudoirs, gardens, kitchens, while men still have business careers. Men provide financial and social salvation for women, and women have to trick them into doing so.

Above all, Colette is at pains to persuade us that gender and sexuality are neither 'natural' nor predetermined. This is shown most clearly in *Le Blé en herbe* (The Ripening Seed, 1923), her text of adolescent sexuality, set in the powerfully evoked landscape of Brittany. Phil and Vinca spend holidays here with their respective families, and their close relationship is a composite of many others; they are childhood sweethearts, quasi-siblings, friends. But this year will prove a turning point as Phil embarks on a thrilling but alarming affair with the older, sophisticated Madame Dalleray, whose house, located on a promontory shaped like a lion, is a fitting tribute to her appropriative strength and mastery. Phil welcomes the affair, recognising his chance to attain a tentative manhood, but his first sexual experiences are far from comfortable. He is literally overwhelmed by the claustrophobic if intoxicating atmosphere in her rooms, nauseated by the bitter orangeade he is given to drink and the incense she likes to burn. Adolescent bodies, Colette suggests, are defenceless against the world, particularly when, as in the case of nascent sexuality, their senses are finely tuned into the environment that surrounds them. For Phil, Camille Dalleray's velvety dark rooms are troublingly close to a monster's lair and his much-desired sexual initiation is an ordeal from which he does not escape unscathed. In her presence he is weak and 'paralysé par une de ces crises de fémininité qui saisissent un adolescent devant une femme' (paralysed by one of those crises of femininity which grip an adolescent boy in the presence of a woman). Colette's playful use of the word 'femininity' makes us realise not just the fragility of Phil's attempts to become a man, but the instability of any gender definition of the body. Sexuality is supposed to reinforce the balance of power between men and women, but when bodies meet in the most intimate interrelation, freed from the normal constraints, they simply will not behave the way that culture dictates they should.

Certainly the women in Colette's text reserve some surprises for the unsuspecting males. Phil is anxious to confess his affair to Vinca, but afraid for the loss of her innocence. He is deeply shocked when he finds out that she is already aware of his night-time absences and their implication. He is even more alarmed by her solution, which is to make love to him herself. What is most revelatory about these developments is Phil's misapprehension of Vinca's personality. Written mostly from his point of view, the narrative repeatedly silences Vinca in favour of representing only her bodily gestures and actions. What Vinca thinks and feels increasingly appears to be a mystery to him This is essentially because Phil has always assumed that she is his perfect duplicate. It requires his liaison with Camille Dalleray to shatter his illusions and prove they are quite unknown to each other, and the sexual act they share highlights their separation rather than heals it. Up until now the relationship between Phil and Vinca has been one of unity, but at Vinca's expense. Her difference has been repressed so that she may provide a reflection of Phil; her sexuality, as proved by her final, enigmatic cheerfulness, is misunderstood. But if this final cheerfulness should appear to give her the upper hand, Colette is careful to remind her readers that the battle of the sexes is a never-ending campaign. This text echoes in many ways the biblical narrative of the Fall, in which Adam and Eve lose their innocence in the Garden of Eden. In this original story, Eve, and all women after her, is condemned to desire her male counterpart and *therefore* be subordinate to him. In Colette's narratives desire is inevitably to be feared by a woman, who will always find its effects debilitating.

This is Colette in cautionary mode. The notion of the body as capricious, demanding, exacting, surprising is a recurrent one across Colette's narratives. For Colette the body is the medium of relationship with the world, a set of appetites and desires that are intense, sometimes inexplicable, but often pleasurable too. If we are to locate an authentic sense of femininity in Colette then perhaps it exists in this strong sense of the body. The importance of sensation, of what we feel, lies at the heart of Colette's representation of identity formation. Sensuality, or the body's response to its environment, and sexuality, or the body's response to another body, are the axes by which we coordinate ourselves in the world. But the sense of a socially constructed woman is equally essential to her vision of femininity. In *Le Blé en herbe*, Phil struggles with ambivalence and insecurity, fearing the advent of sexuality at the very moment that he welcomes it, but Vinca is quite differently portrayed. While she undoubtedly suffers from Phil's capriciousness her own sexual development is contained and controlled; without fuss or damage to others she learns the rules of the game and starts to play by them. Colette is quite the sanest writer I have ever come across. She knows that the body exists in constant tension and interrelation with its surroundings, and she understands that this immediate, reciprocal relationship requires monitoring and compromise. Women may be constrained by their social circumstances, but as circumstances change, so do women, too. And women, for Colette, are infinitely better equipped with this chameleon grace than men, perhaps owing to centuries of practice, but undoubtedly thanks to a highly developed instinct for survival.

Breaking down identity: Simone de Beauvoir

If, as I mentioned earlier, Colette had a tendency to play with the borderline between autobiography and fiction, it is interesting to note by contrast the definitive split in Beauvoir's texts between the non-fiction works (autobiographies and philosophical writings) in which Beauvoir speaks with her own strong, liberated, rational voice, and the novels, which frequently feature confused women undergoing profound emotional crises. This is echoed by the difference between the real Beauvoir and her fictional characters. Beauvoir was a formidable role model; an exceptionally talented student, she helped to found the doctrine of Existentialism with her partner of long-standing, Jean-Paul Sartre, and became a famous author and philosopher in her own right. Whenever Beauvoir writes about herself she always communicates a real sense of liberation and control. Nothing seems to constrain Beauvoir, or compromise her freedom, unlike the female protagonists of her novels who are often encumbered and weighed down by husbands, children, parents, even the choices they have made in the past and images they have of themselves. In her autobiographies Beauvoir can sound invincible, which is only right and proper for someone who transgressed gender conventions in her life, work and politics, but in her fiction, and in the sections of *Le Deuxième Sexe* where she speaks with such distaste of female biology, Beauvoir shows that she is not without insight into the trials of being a woman. It is almost as if her status as man's equal requires Beauvoir to banish all the doubts, fears and frustrations of her female condition, but since these are hard to banish altogether, they resurface as the central concern of her fiction. In this context it is particularly interesting that image is so significant in the psyche of Beauvoir's women protagonists. Female characters in her texts are always striving to be the perfect wife, mother, lover, but are repeatedly forced to confront the distance between the shiny surface of the image and the disturbing reality it conceals.

This is notably the case in her last work of fiction, *La Femme rompue* (The Broken Woman, 1968). This is a collection of three long short stories, each of which focuses on a female protagonist attempting to come to terms with a fairly shattering attack on her sense of identity. Beauvoir sets up a reading practice whereby the reader becomes increasingly aware of the self-deluding and false nature of each protagonist's monologue. All her female characters are attempting to justify their behaviour and rebuild a sense of self, but in each case the woman is feeding off delusions and half-truths which prove to be futile and psychically dangerous. Indeed Beauvoir intended these stories to provide salutary political and existentialist lessons to female readers. The last story in the text, which gives the collection its title, concerns Monique, who discovers her husband has been consistently unfaithful. Monique, forced to confront this unpalatable fact, finds her perception of herself and her past life irrevocably altered.

The theme of needing and desiring to be the perfect wife and mother runs strongly through this collection, and Monique is no exception. She has tied her sense of self to an outdated image, and the realisation that her husband does not love her and her daughters do not admire her brings her close to total breakdown. The ending is not a happy one; Monique does not manage to reconcile herself with her family but is left confronting a bleak future: 'La porte de l'avenir va s'ouvrir. Lentement. [...] Je suis sur le seuil. Il n'y a que cette porte et ce qui guette derrière. J'ai peur. Et je ne peux appeler personne au secours' (The door to the future is opening. Slowly. [...] I stand on the threshold. There is nothing but this door and whatever lies in wait behind it. I am afraid. And there is no one who can help me). It is interesting that, for her male counterparts of Existentialism, such a scene would probably provide the start of the narrative, not its conclusion. Existentialism insists on the alienation of the individual regardless of gender, but the narratives by Sartre and Beauvoir reveal significant differences. While Sartre's heroes explore the nature of their isolation, Beauvoir's heroines need to be convinced of it in the first place, with most of 'La femme rompue' devoted to undermining and then sweeping away the web of domestic relations that surround and support Monique.

The story was intended as a philosophical and political object lesson. Beauvoir was amazed (perhaps slightly disingenuously) when, after the serialisation of the story in *Elle* magazine, letters poured in from readers who sympathised with the luckless Monique. In existentialist terms Monique behaves recklessly, refusing to accept her own freedom and choosing instead to define herself in relation to others, denying her own autonomy. In a further act of *mauvaise foi* Monique believes that relationships are static, that she and Maurice can stay the same forever, while Beauvoir knows that every single action carries innumerable consequences and possibilities. Change is inevitable. By remaining passive, inactive and tied to an image of herself dependent on Maurice, Monique is asking for the trouble she gets.

This may seem a little un-sisterly, and indeed Beauvoir's portrayal of Maurice, the adulterous husband, is strikingly sympathetic, but Beauvoir is taking a harsh philosophical line. However, we cannot dismiss the response from the readers of *Elle* so lightly. 'La femme rompue' is also the tale of a woman, programmed to conform to a culturally valid notion of femininity, who is made to suffer for abiding by society's rules. Monique has identified with a gendered ideal and this role has provided her with a sense of identity. Yet Monique is betrayed by Maurice, and not just sexually. His rejection of her suddenly reveals the gap between real and ideal, between image and reality, showing her up as a fraud and, worse still, as a stranger to herself: ' Je me voyais si tranquillement dans ses yeux. Je ne me voyais même que par ses yeux' (I was so content to see myself reflected in his eyes. I only ever saw myself through his eyes). Deprived of her identity Monique must confront what lies beneath the roles she has assumed for so long. What she finds is, precisely, nothing, and the terror of the void, the recognition that there is no one whom she has to be, provides the climax to Beauvoir's narrative.

'La femme rompue' is a tale of its time, a moment in history when women stood on the threshold of change but did not know where the future would take them. Its roots are in existentialism which represented the post-war disorientation of an entire society, but its focus is specifically female, denouncing an ideal of femininity which is perilously close to cliché and which Beauvoir, always a severe critic, reads as a lazy alternative to the trials of identity formation. The notion of a socially constructed woman is clear in her texts, but what is interesting is that Beauvoir lacks a view of 'repressed' femininity. There is no authentic woman struggling to make herself heard. Beauvoir offers no solution to the conundrum of identity, nor does she represent women as victims. She is never less than harsh with her characters, showing their complicity with their gendered ideal as a dead end that should have been avoided.

Re-inventing identity: Marguerite Duras

The texts I have been discussing by Beauvoir and Colette have all been realistic narratives, that is to say texts which represent a world not unlike the one in which we live. The events that occur are plausible, the characters are believable, and the scenes follow one another so seamlessly that we forget the controlling hand of the author guiding us through. This is not the case with the work of Marguerite Duras. Duras began by writing realistic novels, but by 1958 when *Moderato Cantabile* was published she had already developed a style that was entirely unique. Duras's work is not hard to read – on the contrary, it is deceptively simple – but because very little background information or explanation is given, the reader is often obliged to fill in the 'gaps' with guesswork or a leap of imagination. Nor is her structure conventional; her plots tend to be repetitive or circular, ending up where they began and lacking an end point or *dénouement.* For these reasons, Duras was considered for a while as a *nouveau romancier*, but ultimately her work is too individual to be categorised.

Duras offers a highly stylised representation of women that shows them failing to conform to social expectations but equally unable to access their repressed authenticity with any clear success. Frequently the women she portrays function as focal enigmas around whom the story revolves. Often they are the subject of investigation by a man for whom they are a potent sexual object. Duras's women are never less than desirable, but they are also empty, cold, distant. They speak little and often seem on the verge of breakdown, but this makes them fascinating to others who long to know their terrible secrets. They have often been, literally, destroyed by some unknown trauma whose contours and landmarks the text seeks, but fails, to map out. Identity in Duras's texts, then, is very fragile indeed. But unlike Colette and Beauvoir who concentrate on the moment of breakdown, Duras is interested in the difficult process of reconstruction that occurs once the trauma is over.

One of Duras's best known novels, *Le Ravissement de Lol V. Stein* (The Ravishing of Lol V. Stein), provides a perfect example of this. Following the classic Durassian model, Lol V. Stein is something of an oddity, a woman apparently lacking any sense of her existential reality, a kind of living ghost. She does, however, have a significant event in her past, and it is yet another abandonment; a ball at T. Beach where she was abandoned by her lover Michael Richardson in favour of the older, enigmatic Anne-Marie Stretter. The narrative marks out this moment retrospectively as the governing trauma of Lol's existence and the origin of her psychic trouble. The rest of the text is concerned with the strategies Lol adopts to recreate this moment, and the implication is that its re-enactment will somehow bring her peace or understanding. However, to recreate the ball, she needs someone to stand in as her lover, and this role is taken by the narrator Jacques Hold.

The reader does not realise that Hold is narrating until, about a third of the way through the text, he announces his identity to us. Up until this point the reader has assumed he or she is reading an omnipresent account of Lol's history, but now we must reassess all that we have read, realising that it has been no more than a fantasy imagined and told by Jacques. Suddenly we become aware to what extent the subjectivities of Lol and Jacques are bound together. We have only seen her through his eyes, he has only 'witnessed' her trauma through his own imaginings, but whatever the truth may be of the ball at T. Beach, we realise how much Lol needs Jacques to piece her identity together for her. She tells him: 'Je ne peux plus me passer de vous dans mon souvenir de T. Beach' (I can no longer remember T. Beach without you). As Jacques does his best to oblige, the merging of their subjectivities becomes more marked: 'Lol regardait. Derrière elle j'essayais d'accorder de si près mon regard au sien que j'ai commencé à souvenir, à chaque seconde davantage, de son souvenir' (Lol was watching. Standing behind her I tried to mould my gaze so closely to hers that I began, more clearly with each passing second, to remember her memory).

By moving away from a realist model of narrative, Duras conducts some sophisticated analysis on the construction of identity. Duras seems to be implying that the subject's identity is in the hands – or the mind – of the one who witnesses, who watches. We need somebody else to tell us who we are. This is highly seductive, but dangerous, because we abdicate responsibility for our identity. Furthermore, we need narrative – the very process of putting a story together – to make that identity meaningful and comprehensible. Having made these implications, Duras then problematises them by suggesting that, essential as it is, narrative is limited. Particularly in the case of trauma, or other violent, intense, significant moments, narrative lacks the means to portray the event or express its meaning. What we most need to say often lies on the limits of the expressible. Furthermore we must wonder who is in the best position to understand these momentous events. Duras suggests that we need witnesses to tell us what happened in times of crisis, but those witnesses never have an absolute, unmediated access to the mind of the victim. Lol and Jacques, for all their closeness, are no further forward in understanding what happened to Lol. What we end up with in this novel is a series of mental games, a convoluted play of reflections between two individuals who piece together the past with the aid of fantasy and imagination.

At the end of the novel, there is no resolution. The re-enactment of the ball does not achieve the desired result of reconstructing Lol's identity, and there is no advancement of understanding, either of the night itself or the character of Lol. Instead the text implies that yet another repetition is required. The reader is forced to question Lol's need for a 'cure', and wonder whether what she really desires is the very process of interaction between herself and Jacques. Certainly this radical treatment of identity shows how dependent we are on the transient and unreliable support of others, narrative, and imaginative power to understand ourselves.

Narrative experimentation: *écriture féminine*

Duras's experimental text leads us onto the more general issue of innovative writing by women. *Le Ravissement de Lol V. Stein* was written in 1964 at the start of a wave of experimental writing that was linked to the revolution of May 1968, the feminist movement which grew out of it, and a broader, cultural surge of interest in questions of language and its potential for revolutionary power. These questions were fundamental to the antagonism between French and American schools of feminism back in the 1970s and 1980s. Whereas American feminists tended to push hard for new legislation and political consciousness-raising, French feminists felt that nothing would really change until people changed the way that they thought. And changing people's thought patterns required a fundamental review of the way we use and structure language. The political correctness that informs the way we speak nowadays is a direct descendant of these earlier endeavours. At the time, however, the debate in French universities was far more sophisticated, drawing on cultural theorists like Michel Foucault who argued that sexuality was a product of discourse, and psychoanalytic theories which considered the importance of language acquisition to the development of the child.

The argument of French feminists was that language was partiarchal, dominated by the male perspective. This is a difficult concept to understand and better exemplified by some of the precise arguments put forward. Two feminists in particular (who later rejected the term 'feminist' but kept doing what they always did), Hélène Cixous and Luce Irigaray, were at the forefront of linguistic investigation. Cixous developed the concept of *écriture féminine* as an alternative to the dominant discourse (in practice Cixous and Irigaray concentrated on works of literature and philosophy, rather than everyday speech). Both argued that, in the Western world, woman has been denied her specificity in favour of making her into a mirror in which man can see himself reflected, and, in this respect, language functions no differently. To prove the inherent sexism of language, Cixous worked with a set of binary oppositions – light/dark, strong/weak, active/passive – and argued that the couplet male/female could be read as underlying them all, with the negative term always associated with femininity. Cixous saw in this a prime example of the way that femininity functions within discourse, supporting and reflecting the dominant masculine term. Both Cixous and Irigaray rejected the way that language is organised, arguing that women needed to uncover a new discourse, one that would be experimental and innovative, breaking the rules of form and grammar to reach a new linguistic vision of society and culture. Such a language would be *écriture féminine* (or *parler femme* in Irigaray's terms). In her essay 'Le rire de la Méduse', Cixous noted that up until 1975 only three writers had achieved *écriture féminine*: Colette, Duras and Jean Genet. So, theoretically it was considered possible for a man to write in this style.

However, *écriture féminine* is based on an analogy between physical sexual difference and one's relationship to language. Male sexuality that finds its basis in the simplistic progression from erection to ejaculation and detumescence, is aligned with a structure of narrative that is linear, authoritative and end or climax-oriented. Female sexuality, being more diffuse and multiple, is therefore seen to correspond to a style that is more fluid, fragmented and ambiguous. Part of the multiplicity assigned to femininity is understood as stemming from women's capacity to give birth. Maternity is seen as endowing her with an acceptance, totally alien to traditional philosophy, of otherness within identity. The embrace of otherness or doubleness by female bodies, can be seen to result in a form of writing that subverts the organising conventions of narrative. For instance, *écriture féminine* actively promotes multiple, contradictory meanings existing within a single piece of writing. As a writing practice, then, we can identify several conventions that *écriture féminine* seeks to disrupt because they can be read as overly rigid and organising in a 'masculine' way, notably the order and temporality of narrative, and the authority with which meaning is conveyed. Instead, it promotes the exploration of ambiguity and musicality in language, and the discovery of new, more fluid forms of narrative structure.

These are some of the basic elements of *écriture féminine*, but it is clearly not without problems as a concept. Notwithstanding the difficulties of tying narrative format to biological structures, not all women want or try to write this way to express their feminist leanings. Some excellent social realist novels have been written in the latter half of the century by women such as Claire Etcherelli, Christiane Rochefort and Benoîte Groult. Equally, highly lyrical writing by women does not necessarily have clear feminist intent. Colette's sensuous and poetic prose falls into this category, as does the work of her Decadent predecessor Rachilde, and arguably the texts of the *nouveau romancier* Nathalie Sarraute. Many feminists at the time were dismayed to see women's 'subversive' place in writing tied to bodies which, particularly in terms of maternity, were seen as placing political restraints on women. However, if we move away from the more troubled political significance of *écriture féminine* and consider instead the theoretical space experimentation opens up, then it provides a fascinating point of departure for some critical analysis.

Word and body: representation on trial

Although *écriture féminine* was intended as a revolutionary call to arms for women writers to experiment, it would be wrong to suggest such innovation began in the 1970s. In fact it was a fairly seamless continuation of what women had been writing throughout the century. As I have mentioned before, Rachilde, Colette, Duras and Sarraute were all highly innovative writers who preceded, or overlapped with, the feminist movement. Yet it would be true to say that in the 1970s and 1980s experimental texts written by women went further than they had ever done before in their challenge to conventional representation, producing some masterpieces of formal creativity. I shall consider two quite contemporary texts here – *L'Amant* (The Lover, 1984) by Marguerite Duras and *Le Livre de Promethéa* (The Book of Promethea, 1983) by Hélène Cixous – to analyse some of the major preoccupations of this period and the textual dexterity with which they were explored.

Duras's fictional autobiography, *L'Amant*, can be considered a low-level form of *écriture feminine*, less extreme than work by more committed feminist writers, but, for this very reason, easier to understand. It offers an account of her poverty-stricken adolescence in Indo-China and the ostensible focus of the novel is the love affair that Duras, at the age of fifteen, conducted with an older, wealthy Chinese man. But this is also the charting of an equally passionate and aggressive love affair between mother and daughter. Mothers exert an irresistible fascination over the imaginations of modern French women writers, and there is scarcely one who has not engaged with them textually, either in autobiography (Colette's adulatory *Sido* or *La Naissance du jour*, Annie Ernaux's more ambivalent *Une Femme*) or in fiction (Chantal Chawaf's *Blé en sémences* creates a fantasy realm of the mother that is literally made of milk and honey). Issues of maternity and the interpenetration of mother and child may provide new structural possibilities in *écriture féminine*, but they are often explored thematically as well. Love for the mother is never in question in any of these texts, but a coruscating anger caused by stifled independence, neglect and resentment of the enormous importance the mother holds, continually surfaces to trouble the narrative. What is interesting is the strength and tenacity of the mother's influence over the daughter, and what is important for women's literature is the way this influence provides a source of highly creative tension.

The representation of the mother is the foundation of Duras's *L'Amant*, the well-spring from which its creativity flows, and this is mainly due to the overpowering presence of the mother in Duras's mind: 'dans mon enfance le malheur de ma mère a occupé le lieu du rêve' (during my childhood my mother's misery filled the space of my dreams). Duras's mother is neglectful, capricious and angry, partly complicit in her daughter's prostitution, partly infuriated by her developing sexuality. Duras writes as if she inhabited still her child's perspective of the mother, recreating to the point of hallucination this powerfully vibrant and damaging figure. A retrospective reconciliation with her mother is not the aim of this text, however. Rather, Duras feeds off the anger and violence that inhabited this dysfunctional family network, attempting to portray and inhabit – as she does in all her texts – the purest and most intense of emotions.

Duras is fascinated by excess, by extremes of all kind and her work is always an exploration, through the use of an innovative writing style that has earned her an alignment to *écriture féminine*, of the very limits of our experience. For instance, she writes: 'je crois avoir dit l'amour que l'on portait à notre mère mais je ne sais pas si j'ai dit la haine qu'on lui portait aussi et l'amour qu'on se portait les uns les autres, et la haine aussi, terrible, dans cette histoire commune de ruine et de mort qui était celle de cette famille dans tous les cas, dans celui de l'amour comme dans celui de la haine' (I think I've spoken about the love we had for our mother but I don't know whether I've spoken about the hatred we had for her as well and the love that we had for one another and the hatred, too, terrible, in the story that we shared of ruination and death, which was always the story of our family, whether we loved each other or hated each other). I include a lengthy quotation here to show the way that Duras's syntax is distorted by the intensity of the emotions it seeks to convey, the way that love and hate in their violence inhabit the language of the passage, inflicting random attacks on the grammar. *L'amour* and *la haine* repeatedly punctuate the sentence until their coupling seems a kind of inevitability. In fact we could say that Duras is expressing here the way that love and hatred are necessary counterparts in her family history; they are bound together, inseparable in a way that defies understanding and logic, but is nevertheless her personal experience. And, interestingly, this violent love and hatred translates seamlessly into the erotic desire she feels for the Chinese man.

The relationship is partly an act of defiance and rebellion against the mother, but also a way to strike out for much needed freedom and independence. Often the narrator will abandon the 'je' for the third person 'elle', as if the Duras who writes can no longer identify herself with the girl she was. Yet equally to see herself from outside, through the gaze of a desiring male (which is often the position she takes) is to see an image of herself that seems entirely separate from the mother. As we know, she is too caught up with thoughts of her mother, and has difficulty marking the borderline that separates their identities. Although this relationship seems destined to exclude and anger the mother, it will not prove to be the decisive split between them. Instead, as the girl makes love to the Chinese man, she thinks about her mother, talks about her mother, ceaselessly invoking her presence in the room with them. Sometimes she imagines the Chinese man as a parent, thus fantasising a passionate relationship to the mother. Sometimes, by treating him coldly and indifferently she acts as if she *were* her mother. Duras shows how intimate relationships are often crowded with ghosts, spectres from other, troubled relationships that interfere and influence our behaviour. The way that Duras manipulates grammar, abandoning the tidy and contained form of the sentence for looser, internally repetitive phrases is a reflection of this and of a more general lack of belief in any neat and perfect separation of self and other, past and present, love and hatred.

Hélène Cixous's *Le Livre de Promethea* is also the story of a love affair but with significant differences. If Duras's *L'Amant* emphasised the dimension of fantasy and imagination, Cixous's text inhabits it to the exclusion of all other states. It is related in only the most distant way to any kind of social reality (which is one reason why this type of writing is not immediately recognisable as political) and would seem to comprise only the lyrical thoughts of the narrator as she questions who she becomes through loving, and who she becomes through writing about that love. The love object is Promethea, ostensibly a woman but described more as if she were a mythical beast. Promethea is idealised because her womanliness is entirely innocent of any self-consciousness of construction: 'jamais Promethea n'a pensé à dire: "je suis une femme" [...] Non, la vérité c'est: Promethea est' (Never did Promethea think to say: 'I am a woman' [...] No, the truth is: Promethea *is*). Freed from the constraints of time and social context, free entirely from notions of plot, this narrative focuses exclusively on love, writing and identity with the aim of destabilising all the conventions we normally associate with these states.

The narrative begins by exploring the split identity of the narrator. We are told the story involves three people: the 'je' who writes, H and Promethea. 'Je' has decided to take on the writing of the love affair between H and Promethea because 'Depuis une semaine H s'efforce en vain' (For a week H has been trying in vain). There are enough hints to make us think that H stands for Hélène Cixous, but this is never stated. Instead we are to understand that the text is the product of two voices, the H who experiences and the 'je' who writes, and while the difference between them is emphasised, their similarities lead us to suspect that they provide two sides of the same person. Duras's *L'Amant* troubled the rules of autobiography by moving between 'je' and 'elle', yet the reader is always aware that both of these refer to Duras. *Le Livre de Promethea* can only be considered autobiographical by a process of deduction; if H really does relate to Cixous and she is talking about a love affair she has experienced. But the identity of the narrator is profoundly complex. While both positions, 'je' and H, are associated with Cixous, neither can be said to *be* her with any clarity or certainty. 'Je', usually the guarantor of identity, that is to say of one particular presence speaking through the text, becomes instead a position constructed out of convenience and necessity, because *someone* needs to narrate and H, fully occupied with the experience of love, cannot find the words to do so.

The love story at the heart of this text is one between women, but it is again, not about the reality of love as the reader would recognise it. Promethea is an ideal whose perfection seems so impossible (and her perfection here is her 'naturalness' as a woman) that we sometimes have to wonder whether, or in what form, she exists. The narrator adores Promethea because she has something to teach her, and that lesson is all about being a woman. 'C'est comme si je faisais en rêve un cours sur la Liberté' (It's as if I were taking a course on Freedom in my dreams) writes 'je', and given the dream-like state of the text this is quite a realistic summary of it. Returning to the distinction between two kinds of female identity, the socially constructed and the repressed and archaic, we could place this distinction over the characters of je/H and Promethea. We could see the je/H who writes as a self-conscious construction, and the fantasy ideal of Promethea as a pure kind of spontaneous femininity. The aim of this text would be to bring them together through love in a way that merges them but also respects their differentiation. This is a beautiful, lyrical, confusing, sophisticated text that challenges the reader at all times while remaining continually rewarding. Yet it is written outside of space and time as we know them, implying that this ideal coupling of two types of femininity is still no more than a dream.

Women's writing throughout the century has been a rich and fascinating exploration of identity and its expression through language, with the sophisticated twist in more contemporary texts of that language being considered as a foreign ('masculine') tongue, which must be manipulated in new ways if woman's condition is to be articulated. Over the course of the twentieth century, women have become increasingly visible and increasingly vocal and their work continues to refine and develop the imaginative reorganisation of the boundaries between self and other, fantasy and reality, sexuality and domination that they have challenged so creatively.

Suggested reading

Diana Holmes, *French Women's Writing 1848-1994* (London: Athlone Press, 1996). Excellent and wide-ranging introductory guide with a highly lucid chapter on *écriture féminine*.

Diana Holmes, *Colette* (London: Macmillan, 1991). Comprehensive and clear, this guide covers Colette's entire works.

Elizabeth Fallaize, *The Novels of Simone de Beauvoir* (London & New York: Routledge, 1988). Clear and informative study of Beauvoir's fictional work.

Toril Moi, *Feminist Theory and Simone de Beauvoir* (Oxford: Blackwell, 1990). Particularly strong on reading the feminist and existentialist elements of Beauvoir's texts.

Leslie Hill, *Marguerite Duras. Apocalyptic Desires* (London & New York: Routledge, 1993). A challenging but rewarding guide to Duras's work.

6

Trauma, Myth and Memory:

Making History Personal

The twentieth century has ended so recently that it is difficult to look back over its final decades with anything like an objective overview. But if we compare daily life now with life at the beginning of the century, we can see that modern culture is distinguished by its extraordinary degree of sophistication. Developments in technology, science and medicine mean that we know more about our bodies and our world than at any other point in history. With the rise and rise of the media and the popularisation of culture by television and cinema, we have more opportunities and more ability than ever to analyse the knowledge we possess and our relationship to it. I think it is fair to say that European culture has never been so self-aware. And yet the mysteries of the human heart remain unsolved. Happiness proves continually elusive. The old hardships of poor medical care, widespread poverty and women's oppression may be no more, but new sorrows have come to take their place: stress, trauma, terrorism. The growth over the course of the century of psychoanalysis testifies to the fact that life is a challenge to which we are unequal, and that experience scars. In psychoanalysis, the patient is encouraged to talk at great length, not only about the problems she/he is currently experiencing, but about his/her entire past life, telling the story over and over again until it can be made to make sense, or until the patient has expressed what they were previously unable to say. At the basis of psychoanalysis is the recognition that we are first and foremost creatures of language, and that, faced with the bleak midwinter of suffering, only narrative has a hope of saving us.

It is not surprising, then, that French literature since the 1970s has been distinguished less by distinct literary movements (an indication of the extent to which notions of community have failed) than by any number of poetic voices crying in the wilderness: yes, but what did that mean *for me*? It has also dispensed with any overt interest in the abstract domains of philosophy or pure linguistic experimentation. Instead it has increasingly problematised the notion of a life story, of being able to narrate one's life in a way that expresses authentically the experience of living that life, and in a way that manages to overcome the traumas that history and culture have placed in its path. Partly due to the rise of psychoanalysis, partly due to an advanced theoretical understanding of the effects of literature, narrators in these later texts are self-consciously aware of their need for stories if they are to make sense of their experiences.

Contemporary French texts are still motivated by events of national importance that urgently require exploration. At the end of the century, literature is still haunted by historical traumas from earlier times; the wars, the Holocaust, the bloodshed of decolonialisation. But the perspective which later texts take is one that seeks the moment when History is translated into personal history. These texts dispense with the notion of representing a collectivity (as existentialism tried to do) and concentrate instead on speaking from an individual perspective. In many ways the texts that were written during the last quarter of the century offer an amalgamation of all the great trends that preceded them: a belief that the story of an individual life could offer general enlightenment (Proust), a need to come to terms with the unbearable suffering of the world (existentialism) and the search for a new kind of language that would do justice to a new kind of reality (experimental literature). These decades also witness a return to (what seemed like) old-fashioned story-telling, as a reaction to the plot-less texts of the *nouveaux romanciers* and *écriture féminine*. However, this story-telling is not without a contemporary twist. Because readers, too, are so much more sophisticated nowadays, elements of the fantastic, the nonsensical and the bizarre that frustrate or complicate reading are often prominent.

There are so many wonderful contemporary texts to choose from. There have been excellent new takes on the detective novel by Patrick Modiano and Jean Echenoz, and imaginative and unusual work by women such as Marie Darrieussecq or Marie Redonnet.

Equally impressive has been the brilliant quirkiness of authors such as Daniel Pennac or Christian Bobin, and the dark, disturbing world of Michel Houllebecq. All these authors are readily available in bookshops or from the internet for any reader keen to expand their horizons. Contemporary French fiction distinguishes itself by its tremendous verve and creativity. At the moment a large number of relatively new authors are producing texts that are full of innovation and originality. There is no real canon that exists for recent work; new authors are rising to prominence all the time and the field for exploration and discovery is wide open. The three texts I have chosen offer only a small taste of all that is available, but they do exemplify the concerns I mention above, are recognised as modern classics, and will be quite unlike anything you have ever read before.

Perec's *W ou le souvenir d'enfance* (1975)

Georges Perec was a member of the experimental group Oulipo (Ouvroir de littérature potentielle), founded in November 1960 to place mathematical constraints on fictional writing in order to foster new forms of literary creativity. For instance, Perec's 1969 novel *La Disparition* (The Disappearance) achieves the amazing feat of never using the letter 'e', while its companion piece *Les Revenents* (Ghosts/Those who Return) uses only that vowel. In some ways his commitment to experimental writing makes him something of a throwback in the context of this chapter. However, the text I will be discussing is such a subtle and unique representation of what it meant to be a Jewish child living in France during the Holocaust, and such an unusual kind of autobiography, that it is a perfect example of an engagement with History that results in thoroughly modern literature.

W ou le souvenir d'enfance (W or the Memory of Childhood) is not a straightforward autobiography. To begin with, it is a split narrative in which two storylines alternate, one of which is the overtly fictional tale of the fantasy island, W, that is entirely devoted to sporting endeavour (to which I will return). The other narrative does indeed attempt to piece together Perec's childhood, but it opens with the disclaimer: 'je n'ai pas de souvenirs d'enfance' (I have no memories of my childhood). This is because Perec's early years have been dominated, overtaken in fact, by the Second World War. His father is killed in battle, his mother is deported, Perec as a Jew is removed to various safe houses and he is eventually adopted by his father's sister after the war. Half the narrative will be devoted to sifting through the few pieces of documentary evidence that he owns: some photos, some real locations he has visited, a few memories that almost without exception turn out to be fabrications or deformations, and the meagre information that his family grudgingly supply. Perec's narratives often adopt a tone that is almost coldly clinical, and despite the potentially emotive subject matter, this text is no exception. When talking about the shreds of his past that still remain, for instance, the photos he possesses of his parents, it is this lack of emotion that is striking. The descriptions we get are more like official reports than creative writing. He focuses on the minutiae that make up the representation; the clothes that the figures are wearing, the exact poses in which they are standing, Perec's childishly over-large ears get repeated mention. Readers wait patiently for an explanation of what these photos mean to Perec, how he feels when viewing the parents he so tragically lost, but for such personal details they wait in vain.

In fact our expectations of what an autobiography is, of what it intends to do, are constantly confounded. A more traditionally oriented autobiography would not be disconcerted either by partial amnesia or by a lack of material evidence of the past. We would expect it instead to assemble its sparse fragments and milk them for meaning and significance, deducing or guessing what cannot be known, filling in the gaps, making those leaps of intuition. Instead Perec's text stacks up fragmented and insufficient memories in order to consolidate the sense of alienation and loss that pervades his writing. Two texts that Perec wrote fifteen years before the publication of *W* are included, one about each parent. Precursors of this larger if no more successful autobiographical project, these are annotated in great detail as Perec literally pulls them to pieces, pointing out the falsifications, the impossibilities and the mistakes that constitute them. There is clearly no attempt at self-comfort here. Rather Perec wants to be sure that he has nothing that he owns of the past. He does not tell us why he wants to be dislocated from his own childhood, but he tells us that the very dislocation is reassuring: 'Cette absence d'histoire m'a longtemps rassuré: sa sécheresse objective, son évidence apparente, son innocence, me protégeaient, mais de quoi me-protégeaient-elles sinon précisément de mon histoire, de mon histoire vécue, de mon histoire réelle' (For a long time this absence of history was reassuring: its dry objectivity, its brute self-evidence, its innocence, protected me. But what, precisely, did it protect me from, if not my own history, the history I'd lived, my authentic history).

Perec's text is playing sly games with the reader. Under the cover of researching his past as if he wanted to recover it, he is in fact burying it ever deeper into obscurity. And yet, for the cautious, careful reader, there are plenty of clues as to the nature of that 'histoire réelle' from which he needs to be protected. For example, he describes a dream-like memory in which, at the age of three, he identifies his first Jewish letter in a magazine. Returning to this memory, he points out that he could not be in the place he thinks he was, that his aunt tells him the magazines were in French, and that the letter he identified does not in any case exist. This is a highly telling anecdote, for the absent Jewish letter is clearly important here. It is not by sheer chance that Perec remembers this incident and remembers it wrongly. The transformation of the Jewish sign from a fundamental one – the first he can read – to an impossible, absent one is very significant. For Perec, existing under a Jewish sign was clearly impossible. Had he admitted to his Jewishness in his early childhood he would, quite probably, have ceased to exist at all, deported and killed like his parents. The absence of his parents and of his memories of them is thus only a focal point for his radically absent origins. The story of his lost Jewish origins is essential to his autobiography, but it is not a story he can tell in any straightforward way, for it recalls a period of his life lived in unexplained danger and fear.

Oddly enough, it is the fictional story of the island of W that will contain the real insight into his childhood. It constitutes the only memory he has from his past, a story he wrote at the age of thirteen and forgot about until one evening in Venice when he remembered it in a moment of almost Proustian recall. Ostensibly the story of W has absolutely nothing to do with his autobiography, yet Perec states: 'dans le réseau qu'ils tissent, comme dans la lecture que j'en fais, je sais que se trouve inscrit et décrit le chemin que j'ai parcouru, le chéminement de mon histoire et l'histoire de mon chéminement' (in the network they weave, as in the reading I make of them, I know can be found inscribed and described the road I travelled, the development of my story and the story of my development). We know, then, that Perec's absence of memory is in some sense protective, and that we have to turn to the story to make sense of his past.

It is in two parts, with the first a frame narrative. The narrator, but not, he tells us explicitly, the hero, is Gaspard Winckler, a deserter whose false identity returns to haunt him when the young child whose papers he has been given disappears in a shipwreck. The story of W, like Perec's autobiography, has more than a touch of the detective novel about it, but if the latter is a tale of lost parents, then W begins as the tale of a missing child. But once Gaspard realises he is expected to find his namesake, lost at sea in the vicinity of some islands, this part of the story is simply abandoned, never to be resolved. From then on the narrative will be concerned with detailing life on W and the tone will be one of a well-written holiday brochure; emotionless, detailed and containing within it the seeds of its own self-parody. Perec uses this tone to excellent effect. It suits our initial impression of an olympian utopia that promotes a healthy, just and idealised society. But as the narrative breaks down to reveal the evil and absurd underside of the island, the black humour and the horror of the text stem from the coolly detached descriptions of W's barbaric practices.

The realisation that W is not all what it seems breaks gradually on the reader, as Perec reveals ever more outrageous regulations to W's sporting life. What could be more meritocratic than an island organised by sporting achievement? Until we realise that those who lose forfeit their meals, while those who win are invited to a champion's banquet from which they will emerge gorged and drunk in the early hours of the morning, ruining their chances of competing on the following day. The system of rules that at first appears so logical and pedantic turns out to be at the mercy of capricious officials. Rules are regularly altered: for instance, headstarts and handicaps are given in a random and arbitrary manner and sometimes the last person to finish will win (although this is not declared until the race is over). On W men and women are segregated, the women and children confined to one housing block. But every so often the women are placed, naked, on the track, allowed a head start and then the men are released from a restraining cage in order to chase and claim (rape) them. What shocks most about the account of W is the dramatic switch from ideal to ordeal, from fascination to horror, from dream to nightmare. That a society should be entirely organised by rules, and that those rules should be so unjust and tortuous touches a raw nerve of outrage in the reader. When we reach the end of the narrative and W has degenerated into a concentration camp, we recognise a horrible kind of logic at work. The abuse of power that motivates a corrupt official is indeed no different to the abuse of power that produced the concentration camps. In both cases, what started out sounding perfectly logical, a simple matter of superiority, becomes a sickening attack on human rights.

The concentration camp message is clear and powerful, but how can we link W to Perec's childhood? Perec himself gave us the clue when he said the answer was woven into the writing itself. If we take away the sporting elements of W and read it as the world of a child, then Perec's perspective becomes clearer. The depersonalised voice he uses to describe the horrors of W points to the regulating, adult voice that must have attempted to normalise the often frightening and grief-stricken circumstances of Perec's young life. The fact that this voice cannot do its job, and that the horror of W becomes apparent nevertheless, is also telling. Equally the breakdown of the regulation of the games on W must indicate a childhood where authority shows itself to be all-powerful but absurd and cruel. There is a desire here to create a system of perfect justice, but such a system cannot be sustained and collapses into its opposite; a world of absolute but arbitrary punishment for the fact of existing and doing what one is told. Also, there is no point in continuing with the adventure story format: lost children are never recovered, there is no possible happy ending. The child that Perec was can never be resurrected from the fragmented traces of the past.

Indeed, one obvious problem in the narrative is the lack of a hero, or of a protagonist to carry any of the stories interwoven here. The anonymity of all the participants in these tales is a striking feature, no more so than on W, where contestants are named after the races they have won. For Perec identity is always in flux, or else non-existent, as in the ultimate symbol of depersonalisation, the nameless, faceless crowd who watch the races but remain unexplained in Perec's otherwise extraordinarily detailed account. The lack of belief in identity, and the emotional emptiness at the heart of this tale, means that Perec's text can be read as a crisis of survival. Perec survived the onslaught of history, but only by abandoning his Jewish identity, by being absent from the genocide of the Second World War, and by failing to be a witness to the unjust deaths of his parents. By rights Perec should have died as well. Instead he survived, but at the cost of abandoning his childhood self. This is a text that dramatises the fear that the cost was too great. Yet it is poignant in many ways that W ends up rejoining reality by revealing itself as a concentration camp. It shows that in writing and creating Perec is never absent from his lost parents; his fate is bound up absolutely with theirs. Ultimately the story of W can be read as a fantasy that creates memories for Perec where there were none, that reveals in the texture of his writing the fear, the horror and the guilt that found no form of representation in his childhood, but were transformed instead into zones of opacity and silence. The fantasy of W provides a bridging narrative, a way of accessing a highly traumatic memory in a coded and disguised form.

Tournier's *Le Roi des Aulnes* (1970)

The next novel to be discussed is also the story of a man's engagement with History, and once again the historical event is the Second World War. The fictional story of Abel Tiffauges, one-time garage mechanic in Paris, could not be more different from Perec's quasi-autobiography, although it also concerns itself with the vulnerability of children and the need to make sense of one's life. Tournier's novels often focus on a quest or a journey of initiation in which ordinary people are caught up and transformed by an astonishing sequence of events linked to a specific cultural or historical context. When I say 'ordinary' I mean that Tournier's protagonists have no reason to expect the adventures they experience, for they are generally powerless, marginalised people. They are also usually flawed in some way; 'ordinary' for Tournier means one half low-life non-entity, one half total lunatic. Yet the perversity his characters often display is represented as complex and worthy of our sympathy, if not our understanding. Generally, perversity is portrayed as an authentic desire for a very different form of sexuality, or spirituality, to the one on offer in contemporary culture, and therefore harmless. That said, Tourner's novels are not for the squeamish or faint-hearted. They are violent, sordid and shocking, never flinching from a full and brutal portrait of mankind.

Yet while they revolt, they nevertheless engage the reader intellectually. The French tradition of incorporating philosophical thought into fictional writing is in evidence in Tournier's work, but seamlessly integrated into the narrative. He achieves this by making reading and the question of interpretation the very philosophical problem the reader must tackle. Tournier is interested in the notion of destiny, or the way that we interpret our life retrospectively as having a pattern, or a trajectory that unwittingly we have had to follow. He therefore highlights the practice of reading that each individual performs on his or her life and the historical situation in which it takes place. To speak of destiny is to be alerted to the degree of subjectivity in such a judgement, but Tournier shows us that any understanding of History is based on an identical kind of interpretation. We cannot live history – be it personal or public – without interpreting the events that occur, by imposing or deducing patterns of meaning that may well be misplaced but are utterly seductive. History invites us to do this, for it is always part fact, tragic, banal or otherwise, and part magic, the serendipity of chance or coincidence. Yet the reader can never be entirely convinced by either the practice or the results of such interpretation. The texts pose problems of interpretation that cannot be solved concerning the absurdity or significance of History, while the reader is forced into ambivalence over the very practice of reading that we cannot but undertake.

In *Le Roi des Aulnes* (The Erl-King), Abel Tiffauges is subject to a series of extraordinary twists and turns of fortune as he becomes caught up in the turbulent political and historical backdrop of the Second World War and the rise of the Nazis. In a long and complex narrative he tells us of his unhappy childhood, his life in Paris, his arrest for paedophilia and his imprisonment in a prisoner-of-war camp. Here his ability to care for animals earns him a job as park ranger for one of Hitler's generals. After another twist of fate, he becomes the leader of one of the training schools for the Hitler Jugend in Prussia. It should be clear already that Tiffauges's destiny is bound up with his relationship to animals and, more significantly, to children. Alarmingly, this relationship is an uneasy mix of compassion and exploitation. Tiffauges experiences a fascination for children that is in part an innocent desire to nurture and protect them, in part a voyeuristic desire for their peachy flesh and their delectable purity. The narrative tracks Tiffauges's development through an exploration of the figure of the ogre, the monster who feasts on the flesh of children. Although the figure of the ogre is held out as a kind of destiny for Tiffauges, it is by no means imposed as a simple determining concept, nor a straightforwardly negative one. We cannot simply mock and revile him, or dismiss him as evil and perverted, and while he continually ends up in situations where the ogre comparison is easy to make, we cannot but recognise that he is more than this. Rather, Tournier's novel shows how inevitable it is for those in authority – even only relative authority – to exploit their power excessively or perversely. He shows us how troubling, sexual undertones can be found in the most seemingly compassionate relationships, and how the vulnerable are always hunted, exploited and betrayed.

The novel begins with the words: 'Tu es un ogre, me disait parfois Rachel. Un ogre? C'est-à-dire un monstre féerique, émergeant de la nuit des temps? Je crois, oui, à ma nature féerique, je veux dire à cette connivence secrète qui mêle en profondeur mon aventure au cours des choses, et lui permet de l'incliner dans son sens' ('You are an ogre', Rachel would say to me sometimes. An ogre? You mean a fantastic monster surging out of the night of time? Yes, I do believe in my fantastic nature. I mean to say I believe in a secret complicity which, in its dark depths, weaves my adventure into the passage of events, and allows them to be altered in my favour). Already in these opening lines the complex thematics of Tournier's work are overlaid one on top of the other. Tiffauges's personal history will correspond, perhaps even dictate the course of world events, and the issue at stake is that of monstrosity, or the place of the ogre in society. Tiffauges will come to represent the ogre in his less than

savoury relations with children, but he will not be alone in his perversity. He will also be representative of his historical time through
his involvement with – and the narrative's portrayal of – Hitler and
his Hitlerjugend.

Much later in the novel when Tiffauges is a prisoner of war he
comes across the tantalising sight of a roomful of naked girl children in the town hall near where he is working. He discovers that
these children are destined for the Hitler youth, and they are
described as Hitler's birthday present. The giving is all one way, however, for the administrator who accompanies him comments with
black irony on: 'l'ogre de Rastenburg [Hitler], qui exigeait de ses
sujets, pour son anniversaire, ce don exhaustif, cinq cent milles
petites fille et cinq cent milles petits garçons de dix ans, en tenue
sacrificielle, c'est-à-dire tout nus, avec lesquels il pétrissait sa chair à
canon' (the ogre of Rastenburg who demanded from his subjects
for his birthday this exorbitant gift: five hundred thousand little
boys and five hundred thousand little girls prepared for sacrifice,
that is to say, completely naked, whose flesh he pummelled with
cannon fire). The figure of the ogre, the devourer of children, rises
up above this text as a powerful symbol of a kind of corrupt
authority that sadistically exploits its power over the vulnerable and
the innocent. A figure who seeks the gratification of a perverse
sexual pleasure in the suffering or even in the destruction of the
child. There are clearly echoes here of the officials on Perec's island
of W, but Tournier's text is far more explicit in its treatment of the
motivations for the kind of violence that resulted in the crimes of
the war.

This text is littered with incidents of extreme violence against
children, most of which are profoundly troubling and disturbing. If
we look in particular at one incident involving Tiffauges there is, I
think, a message about the nature of violence to be extracted. In a
period of his life before the outbreak of war Tiffauges becomes a
keen photographer of children. Out photographing one day he
notices two boys on rollerskates, one of whom has an accident and
hurts himself. Tiffauges rushes to the scene because he is fascinated
by the wound the child has sustained and wants to take pictures of
it. However the child, dizzy still, proves a less than model subject:
' "Il va tomber," prononce l'un des enfants. Il n'en est pas question.

Je le gifle à toute volée. Puis je l'adosse contre le mur' ('He's going to fall over,' one of the children declares. There's no question of that. I slap him hard. Then I lean him up against the wall). Once Tiffauges has his pictures, however, his desire for the child finds a new form of sublimation in helping him, and specifically, in carrying him: 'Je me relève, et mes épaules touchent le ciel, ma tête est environné d'archanges musiciens qui chantent ma gloire. [...] C'est la seconde fois en peu de mois que j'enlève dans mes bras un enfant blessé et que l'extase phorique m'enveloppe' (I stand up and my shoulders touch the sky, my head surrounded by an orchestra of archangels singing my glory [...] This is the second time in as many months that I have carried a wounded child in my arms, and been overwhelmed by phorical ecstasy). In neither of his responses to the wounded child can we detect a straightforwardly compassionate or disinterested stance. Tiffauges's perverse sexuality is apparent in both his sickening disregard for the child's injuries and then in the spiritual bliss he enjoys when carrying him.

I will return to the notion of carrying a child, but let us consider first the violence he employs, slapping the child to make him stand up. Tiffauges can treat the child this way because he ignores or denies, or simply does not recognise the child's subjectivity. The child is after all referred to as The Child, an interchangeable symbol, just another possiblity of satisfying Tiffauges's intense desire. Who he is, is irrelevant. This is one way, not of justifying violence, but of explaining how it can take place at all. Violence is based on a denial of the other's difference, a denial of their worth or of their uniqueness. The narrative draws an implicit parallel between Tiffauges's complex combination of desire, neglect and exploitation, and the Hitler youth movement, in which thousands of boys and girls, nameless, faceless but perfect and interchangeable, are turned into cannon fodder. The focus on the child here is significant. The violence inflicted on children in this novel is powerfully revolting: revolting in the sense of nauseating, but also in the sense of effecting an outrage, an ethical offence. Children embody a special kind of purity that demands our protection, yet they are also easily grouped together, easily preyed upon. Children are a natural target for violence, being in a permanent state of submission, but because it is difficult to stomach violence against children, such acts demand that we rethink the power of those in authority.

Returning to the incident, Tiffauges, who has been bigger and older enough to slap the child and force him to submit to his will, now shows how being bigger and older means he can carry the child and help him. This is and is not disinterested. That is to say, it is in the act of selfless love for the child that Tiffauges will come to find redemption. The narrative will not represent Tiffauges as simplistically monstrous, or at least this tale asks us to rethink the concept of the monster as someone who is *surhumain*, in the sense of being somehow overdeveloped or excessive. Tiffauges embodies excess in his complicated relationship to children, for his love is both paedophilic *and* maternal. To carry a child and, in French, *porter un enfant*, means both to lift it up and also to carry it in pregnancy. To carry a child in this text takes on a condensed symbolic meaning, suggesting when Tiffauges physically lifts a child that he is some sense fulfilling his maternal vocation.

When Tiffauges is called an ogre by his girlfriend, Rachel, at the very start of the narrative, it is in the context of an argument that marks the end of their relationship. Tiffauges reads into this appellation a mystical destiny rather than the frustrated cry of a woman whom he cannot satisfy (he is, he tells us 'microgénitomorphe' – or underendowed). Either way it marks the end of his heterosexual relations and the start of an exploration of a different kind of sexuality, one that bypasses genital sexuality altogether, or indeed any kind of pairing off or relationship. This form of sexuality is bound up with a fantasy Tiffauges has of a kind of androgynous wholeness. He reconsiders the biblical story of Adam and Eve, arguing that man's fall occurs long before the incident with the apple. Rather it is the very creation of Eve that destroys man's originary unity. Tiffauges confesses to a form of nostalgia for this mythical being:

> On n'echappe pas à la fascination plus ou moins consciente de l'Adam archaique [...] perpetuellement en proie à des transports amoureux d'une perfection inouïe – possédant-possédé d'un même élan – si ce n'est sans doute – et encore qui sait! – pendant les périodes où il se trouve enceinte de ses propres oeuvres. Alors quel ne devrait pas être l'équipage de l'ancêtre

fabuleux, homme porte-femme devenu de surcroît porte-
enfant, chargé et surchargé, comme ces poupées gigognes
emboîtées les unes dans les autres.

(It is impossible to escape a more or less conscious fascination
with this archaic Adam, perpetually prey to amorous trans-
ports of an unimaginable perfection – possessed and possessor
in the same movement – if, of course, he is not – and then
again, who knows! – in one of the periods where he finds himself pregnant by his own hand. What, then, must the internal
organisation of this fabled ancestor be like, man as woman-
container who has become in addition a child-container, filled
and overfilled, like a set of Russian dolls, one inside another.)

Tiffauges's fantasy, expressed here in Tournier's typically lush and
evocative prose, is a good example of the way that Tournier returns
to, and rewrites, cultural myths in order to bring them alive again in
contemporary culture. It is also a good example of the blend of
myth, mysticism and reality that characterises Tournier's texts and
makes them such a queasy brew. The hermaphrodite image is a
medical improbability and its description veers towards the
unpleasant, yet it is impossible not to visualise such a self-sufficient
Adam and be seduced into wondering about its implications. These
rich and paradoxical implications are in fact explored as the 'destiny' of Tiffauges's development. Tiffauges's relationship with
children aims to uncover a masculine form of maternity in carrying
children, picking them up and lifting them to safety, and although
on many occasions Tiffauges's relationship to children is question-
able, the novel ends with his death as he attempts to rescue a child.

We can identify a very peculiar gender politics at work in this
novel, a weaving together of the roles of men and women, mothers
and fathers, to create a highly original composite. However, this is
not a didactic text that offers us a gender transgressing hero in the
figure of Tiffauges. The notion of an original, whole Adam who
could be at once man, woman and child is an impossible fantasy,
and Tiffauges's attempts to embody the feminine result in a man
who both cares for children and desires them, an uneasy and troubling combination of roles. In its concern with the relationships of

dominance and submission, sexuality and innocence that bind adults and children, this text explores some cultural taboos that still have the power to shock and disgust. But Tournier's text excels in refusing us an easy and morally satisfying response to such difficult issues. Tournier's novel considers the blackest side to authority in its depiction of the Nazis and some of Tiffauges's excesses, and yet equally in Tiffauges we find a loving maternal nurturing that is elevated to the status of a religion. There is no easy position from which to read Tournier's representation of perverse compassion and cruel authority, and Tiffauges's death, sinking into the marsh as he carries the frail body of the Jewish child, Ephraim, on his shoulders, is a moment of tragic but mystical redemption. At this moment he is more than a mother or a father, and more than their disturbing composite; he is something else altogether, beyond these hierarchies of love and power.

Djebar's *Les Femmes d'Alger dans leur appartement* (1980)

My final text is again an interweaving of the themes of war, vulnerability and the relentless sweep of History. However it is distinguished, not just from the other works in this chapter but from all the other texts I have discussed, by being Francophone in origin. The term 'francophone' refers to works written in lands other than France where French is the official language, for instance west Africa, Quebec and the Maghreb. Francophone writing began to infiltrate the French literary market in the 1960s, thanks in part to the support and publicity it received from established writers such as André Breton and Sartre. It has become increasingly studied by European and American academics since the 1980s, attracted by the combination of lyrical, rich, often savage prose, and issues of colonialism, slavery, and war. The difficulties of forging cultural and national identities in occupied lands have even resulted in a specific branch of critical theory.

Francophone literature concerns itself fundamentally with cultural spaces, with the way we map out the territories we inhabit, marking out borderlines between nations that are arbitrary but then guarded and patrolled. Even more significant is the way we then invest the space between those borders with ideology. Ideology is complex to explain, but it constitutes a kind of cultural religion that determines what we believe to be possible and acceptable in the way we behave and the organisation of our social life. The difficulty with ideology is that it pervades our patterns of thinking to such a degree that we fail to recognise its presence at all. It blinds us to the possibilities of thinking differently or otherwise so that our culture appears absolutely 'natural', until, that is, war or revolution disturbs its invisible hold. The work of Assia Djebar concentrates on a culture whose ideology is in crisis. Djebar is writing of a community traumatised by the Algerian War of Independence (1954-62) and seeking to reconstitute itself in an authentic, post-colonial way; a way, in other words, that aims to cohere a society split by decades of colonial oppression and, in consequence, by the imposition of social, cultural and religious structures that were not its own; a way that remains true to the traditions of the past while moving forward into the future. Algerian literature charts not only the dying light of colonial oppression by France, but the struggle for the ideological colonisation of the now unformulated and unregulated spaces left behind. Djebar's particular concern in this text is the role that women should play in this society, for their social condition is one that would still shock their Western counterparts.

Les Femmes d'Alger dans leur appartement (Women of Algiers in their Apartment) is a historically specific text that stands on the brink of huge cultural changes. At the time of its writing, Algerian women under the tradition of Islam were confined to their domestic spaces and only allowed out once a week, often at night, to visit the baths. If a woman did venture onto the streets then it was under the protection of a veil that left only one eye uncovered. The protection was for the unsuspecting males in the outside world; in Islamic culture a woman's gaze is powerfully and potently sexual and must be regulated, that is to say, hidden away or, perhaps more aptly, imprisoned. During the war of Independence, however, French authorities encouraged women to go without veils in the hope of undermining Islamic tradition. The consequence was that those women who unveiled mainly joined the Algerian forces and became resistance fighters. This was not what France intended, and a mixed blessing, to say the least, to the traditionalists in Algeria. The impact of these women sleeping rough, fighting, being injured and being killed alongside the men, cannot be underestimated in a society where women were not usually allowed out of doors. Once the war was over, the battle of the sexes continued, with Islamic authorities insisting that women return to what Djebar calls being 'buried alive', or incarceration within their own domestic space. In many ways the war over the borderlines of colonial France was echoed and reiterated by the struggle between male and female universes in post-colonial Algeria.

Les Femmes d'Alger is a collection of short texts that is content to depict this post-colonial culture with honesty and compassion and without explicit judgement. It shows a society that is confused and in transition, but relieved at least to be finished with war, and to be free. Djebar's text focuses mainly on domestic scenes, everyday problems, burials, friendships, the experience of solitude, suffering and illness. There are a number of reasons for representing such seemingly quotidian matters, the most significant being that domestic space is a highly charged ideological battlefield. Families provide the arena in which traditions are handed down, ethics are instilled in children, and the gender culture of a society reproduced in a microcosm. In consequence, when the great changes that history makes eventually filter down to the level of the individual, the experience of the family, or of a small community, provides a yardstick by which real cultural change can be measured. Perhaps even more important for Djebar, domestic space is the province of women, and by speaking of it she reinstates women in history, showing them to be not just victims, but agents of resistance and change, the handmaidens of cultural tradition, but also ready and more than willing to embrace the modern and the new. The women represented in this text (and I am specific here because Djebar's female protagonists have changed with their culture over the past twenty years) stand in limbo, in between a past they have not yet left and a future they are not yet allowed to possess. The gap between old and new is so large that the ideology of how a woman should behave is still to be formulated. For this reason Djebar is able to depict a wide range of women, some working, some still tied to the home, some without veils, some keen to protect the legacies of the past, some old, some young, and many who are scarred, mentally or physically, by the war. The result is what critics have called a 'mosaic', a series of fragments that together make up a detailed and evocative picture of a community of women that up until now has been hidden away and silenced.

The very fact that Djebar speaks of these women is in itself highly significant. Islamic tradition also regulates women's speech. When they speak, women may only speak in whispers, only the elderly have any right to speech at all (the young must wait their turn in the hierarchy) and more significantly still, I think, a woman may only refer to herself 'anonymously'. It is forbidden for a woman to use the first person pronoun; to speak saying 'I'. In one particularly telling anecdote, Djebar talks about the way young girls are instructed in 'le culte du silence qui est une des plus grandes puissances de la société arabe' (the cult of silence, which is one of the greatest weapons of power in Arab society). Djebar calls this 'une seconde mutilation' (a second mutilation), the first being the veil which prevents the woman from seeing. She tells how the dislocation of women from speech is achieved with sometimes ingenious means. When a young girl accepts an offer of marriage the law decrees that she must say 'yes', but since she cannot be seen by her potential bridegroom she must therefore use a male intermediary to speak for her. Djebar points out that this all too often leads to a woman being forced into an undesired alliance, particularly when, given her 'pudeur' (modesty), her tears or her silence can also be read as an acceptance.

Djebar recalls one Persian tradition whereby the young woman is kept behind a curtained door in an adjacent room to that containing her suitor. When the necessary 'yes' is required the women who accompany her hit her head against the door so that she cries out: 'Ainsi, le seul mot que la femme a à prononcer, ce "oui" à la soumission, sous couvert de bienséance, elle l'exhale malaisément, sous l'effet d'une douleur physique ou par l'ambiguité de larmes silencieuses' (Thus the only word that the woman has to pronounce, this 'yes' of submission, she expels with difficulty, under the cover of etiquette; provoked by physical pain or inferred from the ambiguity of silent tears). Djebar shows here that some traditions are better left in the past, and that some communities of women are obliged to be less than sisterly. The main point here is the silence that surrounds the women of Islam which Djebar breaks with her text. By writing about women she opens the door to a cloistered world that has long been invisible, removed from the cultural gaze, even if intrinsic to that culture. Yet in speaking for the women who are silent, Djebar is turning her back on her own traditions, committing a revolutionary act of gender politics, and angering many among her culture. When Djebar published her first novel at the age of 21 she changed her name, birth date and appearance in the hope of keeping the novel secret from her family (they found out nonetheless), indicating her own recognition of the cultural crime she was committing. Furthermore, although Djebar is Algerian, she was brought up in the French education system and she writes in French. To tell the story of the native women of Algeria, she effectively expatriates herself in a foreign tongue. Worse still, the language she uses is at this point in time associated with the enemy.

Although it is in no way a solution to the betrayal of her traditions, it is significant that Djebar's novel is highly polyphonic, which is to say it contains a number of different voices within it. The voices of peasant women combine with those of educated women, colloquial Berber terms are contained in the same space as quite academic analysis, and Djebar distorts the cadences of classical French with the rhythms of local dialect. If the religious battle between the sexes is in some ways an echo of violent conflict over the territories of Algeria and France, the multiple, fragmented voices in Djebar's text, existing intermingled and without hierarchy, must in some way provide a harbinger of the post-colonial society that Algeria seeks to create.

Djebar engages with her country's cultural history in order to understand better the context in which women have to forge a new social condition, and she does so with a strong desire to integrate the most valuable elements of women's past oppression. This may sound a contradiction in terms, but Djebar seeks above all to protect the very sense of community among women about which she writes; a community that has grown out of enforced imprisonment, but one which nevertheless offers security, strength and companionship. She even warns 'la jeune fille aujourd'hui qui emancipe' (the young woman of today who seeks emancipation) for whom 'l'éloignement revient à déplacer le lieu de son mutisme: elle troque le gynécée et la communauté ancienne contre un face-à-face souvent fallacieux avec l'homme' (distance simply ends up displacing the arena of her silencing: she barters the sisterhood and the traditional community for a one-to-one with a man that is often a mistake). Djebar's text is revolutionary in its subject matter, in the stance it takes towards women's rights, in the very act of being written, but it is never propaganda. Djebar does not presume to tell the women of her society what to do; it is sufficiently presumptuous to have spoken for them. But she offers a vision, composed of many small, heterogeneous fragments of a society that contains many possible future societies within it.

So literature at the end of the century is still doing what literature has always done: effecting its own revolutions through its ability to create a new world or to recreate the old one in a way undreamed of before. Contemporary texts unite the ruthless, unstoppable force of History with the vulnerability and isolation of the individual, making history personal while they show the making of personal history.

Suggested reading

Stella Béhar, *Georges Perec: Écrire pour ne pas dire* (New York & Bern: Peter Lang, 1995). In French. A wide-ranging appreciation of Perec's works that provides interesting interpretations.

David Gascoigne, *Michel Tournier* (Oxford: Berg, 1996). Thematic study of Tournier's works that is provocative and sophisticated.

Michael Worton (ed.), *Michel Tournier* (London: Longman, 1995). An edited collection of readings of Tournier's works adopting unusual but insightful perspectives.

Belinda Jack, *Francophone Literatures: An Introductory Survey* (Oxford: Oxford University Press, 1996). An excellent introductory guide to a wide variety of works from different Francophone countries.

Rafika Merini, *Two Major Francophone Women Writers, Assia Djebar and Leila Sebbar: A Thematic Study of their Works* (New York & Bern: Peter Lang, 1999). One of the first in-depth and comprehensive studies of these writers' work.

Conclusion

There is a text by the contemporary writer Marie Cardinal entitled *Le Passé empiété*, in which a woman attempts to come to terms with the near-fatal accident to her children by embroidery; as she sews, she remembers, and thus she renews the bonds with her past, her parents and her childhood. Significantly she uses back stitch, the *passé empiété* of the title, as the main component of her work, declaring: 'on empiète dans le passé pour se lancer dans l'avenir' (one moves back into the past/stitches backwards in order to thrust forwards into the future), going over and over the old stitches, 'en rebrodant par-dessus le travail du commencement, parfois à plusieurs reprises' (embroidering over the earlier work, occasionally several times). The movement of the stitch is read here as having figurative implications for the work of memory, in the way it endlessly moves backwards over the past, sometimes rewriting it in that act of reconsideration. We need to understand the past before we can move forwards into the future.

If the back stitch becomes a figure for memory in Cardinal's texts, it is also a figure for the act of writing, too. As we have seen in so many of these twentieth-century texts, writing has repeatedly traced a return to the past, with the intention of enlightening or consoling the narrator, and of situating them in some significant way in relation to their life, their culture or their history. At the same time twentieth-century texts have often displayed the need to return to the very traditions of literature, in order to unpick them and work over the top in new, experimental forms.The return to the past in the modern age is by no means sterile. Instead it has been consistently seen as a way to move forwards more effectively and creatively, and the very act of retelling the past has often engendered innovation and originality in writers.

Difficult as it is to give an overview of a century that has only just finished, it certainly seems that, at the heart of this progressive age, there is an overriding fascination with retrospection, as if culture and history have been moving so fast, we need to keep looking back to be sure of what happened. Where literature will go in the twenty-first century is anyone's guess, but the emphasis on innovation and creativity seems unlikely to change, and the sophistication of texts and readers alike will only increase. We can at least be sure that the future of literature will mirror its past, and be continually rewritten and reinvented by the hands of the next generation.

Glossary of Authors

Adamov, Arthur (1908-70). Dramatist whose theatrical works with a political slant include *Paolo Paoli* (1957).

Alain-Fournier (pseudonym of Henri Alban Fournier, 1886-1914). Novelist famous for *Le Grand Meaulnes* (1913), a prime example of the poetic novel in the pre-war years, fusing the themes of imagination, nostalgia and adolescence.

Althusser, Louis (1918-90). Marxist critic best known for his conceptualising of ideology as a lived cultural practice.

Angot, Christine (b. 1959). Angst-ridden autobiographical writer, whose experimental texts have risen to prominence on the contemporary scene.

Anouilh, Jean (1910-87). Dramatist of the inter-war years. Creates an artificial stage world dominated by showy make-belief, in which protagonists obsessed with purity are ritually defeated (*Antigone*, 1944, *L'Alouette*, 1953).

Antelme, Robert (1917-90). His work of autobiography and theory, *L'Espèce humaine*, recounted his time in a concentration camp and continues to have a profound impact on war studies.

Apollinaire, Guillaume (pseudonym of Wilhelm de Kostrowitsky, 1880-1918). Poet of great significance and influence. His poetry is a dramatic intermingling of tradition and innovation (*Alcools*, 1914), literature and painting, and the experimental pictogram (*Calligrammes*, 1918).

Aragon, Louis (1897-1982). One of the founders of the Surréaliste group, Aragon was an exponent of a new, unstructured form of writing (*Le Paysan de Paris*, 1926) and an accomplished poet (*Les Yeux d'Elsa*, 1942).

Arrabal, Fernando (b. 1932). One of the later dramatists of the *théâtre de l'absurde* movement.

Artaud, Antonin (1896-1948). Well-known for his theory of *théâtre de la cruauté*, which subsequently influenced a generation of playwrights. His own plays, e.g. *Le Cenci*, are rarely produced.

Aymé, Marcel (1902-67). Novelist and short story writer whose writing combines fantasy and ironic humour and whose body of work has been described as a twentieth-century human comedy.

Barbusse, Henri (1873-1935). Novelist whose portrait of the Great War (*Le Feu*, 1916) combined realism and pacifism to become a great commercial and critical success.

Baroche, Christiane (b. 1935) Novelist with a particular interest in women's identity and issues of maternity (*L'Hiver de beauté*, 1987).

Barrault, Jean-Louis (1910-94). Actor, director and producer acclaimed for his experimental, collaborative theatre.

Barthes, Roland (1915-80). Cultural critic whose influential theories on reading, writing and subjectivity spanned structuralist (*Le Degré zéro de l'écriture*, 1953) and post-structuralist thought (*Le Plaisir du texte*, 1973).

Bataille, Georges (1897-1962). Philosopher, critic and novelist, infamous for his text of violent pornography, *Histoire de l'oeil* (1928; 'new version', 1940).

Baudrillard, Jean (b. 1929). Post-modern critic of contemporary society and the media (*La Société de consommation*, 1970, *Les Stratégies fatales*, 1983).

Beauvoir, Simone de (1908-86). Philosopher and novelist, whose lengthy analysis of the female condition, *Le Deuxième Sexe* (1942), caused uproar on publication and has influenced the global feminist movement. Her novels have also resulted in much acclaim: *Les Mandarins* won the Prix Goncourt in 1954.

Beckett, Samuel (1906-89). Novelist and playwright, writing in both English and French, Beckett's *En Attendant Godot* (1948, performed 1952) remains one of the classic works of the *théâtre de l'absurde*.

Ben Jelloun, Tahar (b. 1944). Moroccan novelist and poet who won the Prix Goncourt in 1987 with his novel *La Nuit sacré*, a companion text to *L'Enfant du sable* (1985) which delves into the psyche of a girl brought up as a boy and her subsequent reaffirmation of female identity.

Benveniste, Emile (1902-76). Structuralist critic working with theories of language.

Bergson, Henri (1859-1951). Philosopher whose enquiries into time and memory influenced Proust.

Bernanos, Georges (1888-1948). Novelist whose work explored Catholic themes, notably *Journal d'un curé de campagne* (1936).

Blais, Marie-Claude (b. 1939). Fiercely satirical novelist from Quebec, attacking the notion of family life and its values (*Une Saison dans la vie d'Emmanuel*, 1965).

Blanchot, Maurice (b. 1907). Literary and philosophical essayist and novelist (*L'Espace littéraire*, 1955).

Blin, Roger (1907-84). Influential theatre director particularly known for his staging of Jean Genet's *Les Nègres*.

Bobin, Christian (b. 1951). Novelist whose texts combine fantasy, fairytale and myth (*Isabelle Bruges*, 1992).

Bonnefoy, Yves (b. 1923). One of the great contemporary poets (*Du mouvement et de l'immobilité de Douve*, 1953; *Rue Traversière*, 1987; *Ce qui fut sans lumière*, 1987).

Boudjedra, Rachid (b. 1941). Algerian writer whose texts return obsessively to explore women's sexual neuroses (*La Répudiation*, 1969).

Bourdieu, Pierre (b. 1930). Founder of the study of the sociology of knowledge, whose work considers the very structures of academic understanding (*Homo academicus*, 1984).

Braque, Georges (1882-1963). Cubist painter whose work influenced avant-garde writers.

Brasillach, Robert (1909-45). Novelist and essayist whose Fascist views led to his trial and execution after the Second World War.

Breton, André (1896-1966). Key founder of the Surréaliste group of artists, Breton married politics, psychoanalysis and experimental literature in poetry (*Les Champs magnétique*, 1920) and novels (*Nadia*, 1928).

Butor, Michel (b. 1926). Allied to the novelists known as the *nouveaux romanciers*, he explored the representation of time and space in narrative (*La Modification*, 1957; *Emploi du temps*, 1956).

Calle, Sophie (b. 1953). Installation artist whose texts and photographs since the 1980s challenge the divide between public and private, art and life.

Camus, Albert (1913-60). Novelist (*L'Étranger* 1942; *La Peste*, 1947), playwright (*Caligula*, performed 1945) and philosopher (*Le Mythe de Sisyphe*, 1942) whose theories of the absurd aligned him with existentialism. He won the Nobel Prize in 1957.

Cardinal, Marie (1929-2001). Best known for her autobiographical fictions which consider the role of women in society, such as *Les Mots pour le dire* (1975), which recounted her successful psychoanalytic treatment.

Céline, Louis-Ferdinand (pseudonym of Louis-Ferdinand Destouches, 1894-1961). Prolific novelist notorious for his pro-fascist sympathies. His dark and disturbing *Voyage au bout de la nuit* (1932) remains one of the great novels about the First World War.

Cendrars, Blaise (pseudonym of Frédéric Sauser, 1887-1961). Experimental poet contemporary to Apollinaire. He worked in conjunction with artists such as Sonia Delaunay.

Césaire, Aimé Fernand (b. 1913). Revolutionary Martinique poet. His *Cahier d'un retour au pays natal* (written 1935, published in Paris, 1939) was championed by André Breton in 1943 and its subsequent republication made him one of the first Francophone writers to arouse considerable interest.

Chamson, André (1900-83). Exponent of the *roman rustique* which sought to reconnect post-war France with the values and harmonies of its mythic, rural heritage.

Char, René (1907-88). Innovative, sophisticated poet whose work was initially influenced by Surrealism but remains resolutely original (*Fureurs et mystères*, 1948).

Chawaf, Chantal (b. 1943). One of the writers aligned to the *écriture féminine* form of writing, Chawaf has had a long and varied career as a novelist producing, among others, works of maternal fantasy (*Blé de semences*, 1976) and vampirism (*Rédemption*, 1989).

Chedid, Andrée (b. 1920). Poet, novelist and playwright whose work, mainly set in Egypt, combines social realism with elements of myth to explore women's experience (*L'Autre*, 1968).

Cixous, Hélène (b. 1937). Novelist, playwright and theorist whose concept of *écriture féminine* influenced a generation of women writers. Her texts (*Jours de l'an*, 1990; *Le Livre de Prométhéa*, 1983) are widely studied and researched.

Claudel, Paul (1868-1955). Dramatist whose work in the 1930s and 1940s

(*Le Soulier de satin*, performed 1943) was aligned to Symbolism. He was fascinated by themes and images of Catholicism and, later, by those of Japanese theatre.

Cocteau, Jean (1889-1963). Stylish commercial playwright and novelist of the 1920s. A leading avant-garde figure whose writing mixes experience and imagination, dream and reality, truth and fiction (*Les Enfants terribles*, 1929).

Cohen, Albert (1895-1981). Autobiographical novelist focusing on aspects of Jewish life and identity, with emphasis on love and politics (*Belle du seigneur*, 1968).

Colette, Sidonie-Gabrielle (1873-1954). One of the greatest and best-loved women writers of the century, her work included fictional autobiographies (*Sido*, 1929; *La Naissance du jour*, 1928), novels (*Le Blé en herbe*, 1923; *Chéri*, 1920) and many short stories.

Condé, Maryse (b. 1937). Guadeloupian writer whose bestselling novels (*Heremakhonon*, 1976; *Moi, Tituba, sorcière*, 1986) explore issues of race through a lyric exposition of history and folklore.

Constant, Paule (b. 1944). Contemporary writer whose novels, many of which are set in Africa, focus on childhood and issues of girl's education (*White Spirit*, 1989). She recently won the Prix Goncourt for *Confidence pour confidence* (1998).

Darrieusecq, Marie (b. 1969). Writer whose recent novels exploring female identity and experience, including *Truismes* (1996), which recounts the tale of a woman metamorphosed into a pig, have catapulted her to literary prominence.

Deguy, Michel (b. 1930). Experimental post-war poet in whose work language and play take centre-stage as he seeks ways to fuse poetry and poetic theory (*Actes*, 1966).

Delaunay, Robert (1885-1941) and **Sonia** (1884-1979). Experimental painters whose work, influenced by Cubism, was termed Orphism by Apollinaire. In the pre-war period they linked their painting productively to poems by Rimbaud and Cendrars as well as Apollinaire.

Delbo, Charlotte (1913-85). Writer whose series of autobiographies detailing her concentration camp experience provide a welcome, if harrowing, female perspective.

Deleuze, Gilles (1925-95). Radical philosopher considering the post-postmodern condition with particular interest in structures of power and politics.

Derrida, Jacques (b. 1930.) One of the most influential philosophers in the twentieth century, his critical practice of deconstruction, which foregrounds the complexity of meaning creation, has been productively appropriated by theorists in a wide range of artistic domains (*L'Écriture et la différence*, 1967; *De la grammatologie*, 1967; *Spectres de Marx*, 1993).

Desnos, Robert (1900-45). Surrealist poet who experimented with hypnosis and automatic writing, and produced collections of punning, subversive, humorous poetry. A member of the Resistance, he died in a concentration camp (*Corps et biens*, 1930).

Despentes, Virginie (b. 1969) Novelist whose disturbing texts of extreme violence and pornography focus on contemporary female society.

Diop, Birago (1906-89). His collection of Black African folktales, *Les Contes d'Amadou Koumba* (1947) provided a significant piece of Francophone literary history.

Djebar, Assia (b. 1936). Algerian writer whose works explore the condition of women and the ideology of domestic space in colonial and post-colonial Algeria (*L'Amour, la fantaisie*, 1985; *Les Femmes d'Alger dans leur appartement*, 1980; *Les Nuits de Strasbourg*, 1997).

Drieu la Rochelle, Pierre (1893-1945). Editor of the prestigious journal *Nouvelle Revue Française*, and novelist whose work fiercely criticised the heroism of war. He was a prominent fascist supporter who committed suicide after the Second World War.

Duchamp, Marcel (1887-1968). Surrealist artist whose paintings, photographs and 'readymades' provided a significant contribution to the movement.

Dupin, Jacques (b. 1927). Contemporary poet whose abrupt, staccato style is reminiscent of René Char.

Duras, Marguerite (1914-96). Experimental writer and film director who has been linked to the *nouveaux romanciers* and to the practice of *écriture féminine*, although ultimately her work remains unclassifiable, original and highly provocative (*Le Ravissement de Lol V. Stein*, 1964; *L'Amant*, 1984).

Echenoz, Jean (b. 1956) Contemporary thriller writer whose novels always provide a stunning twist on the genre (*Lac*, 1989; *Je m'en vais*, 1999, Prix Goncourt).

Éluard, Paul (pseudonym of Eugène Grindel, 1895-1952). One of the most influential Surrealist poets, his poetry focused on themes of love, war and painting (*Capitale de la douleur*, 1926; *L'Amour, la poésie*, 1929).

Ernaux, Annie (b. 1940). Contemporary writer whose autobiographical works explore the relation between life and writing, and her troubled feelings towards her father (*La Place*, 1983) and mother (*Une Femme*, 1988).

Etcherelli, Claire (b. 1934). Novelist best known for *Élise ou la vraie vie* (1967) in which a young woman from the provinces must confront racism and conflict with management on the factory floor.

Fanon, Frantz (1925-61). Uncompromising revolutionary writer, born in Martinique whose *Peau noire, masques blancs* (1952) remains a classic Francophone text.

Foucault, Michel (1926-84). Highly influential cultural historian and theorist whose works focused on the formation of the subject through language and social institutions with particular interest in (among other issues) power, knowledge, madness, sexuality and crime (*Surveiller et punir*, 1975; *Histoire de la sexualité*, vol. 1, 1976).

France, Anatole (pseudonym of Anatole Thibault, 1844-1924). Historical novelist (*Les Dieux ont soif*, 1912) whose interest in the Dreyfus affair led him to denounce anti-Semitism and nationalism in his work, including

Monsieur Bergerat à Paris (1901). He won the Nobel prize for literature in 1921.

Genet, Jean (1910-86). Novelist and playwright who glorified criminality, homosexuality and the suffering of the oppressed (*Les Bonnes*, 1947; *Le Balcon*, 1956; *Notre Dame des fleurs*, 1948).

Genette, Gérard (b. 1930). Structuralist literary critic, concerned with the theory of narratology, or the question of how meaning is produced in texts (*Figures*, 3 vols, 1966, 1969, 1972).

Germain, Sylvie (b. 1954). Contemporary novelist whose poetic texts offer a mixture of magic realism and alternative spirituality. (*Le Livre des nuits*, 1985; *Jours de colère*, 1989).

Gide, André (1869-1951). Prolific and versatile writer whose interest in the conflict between duty and autonomy, and the possibility of sincerity, informed much of his work. His only novel, *Les Faux-Monnayeurs* (1926) is considered to mark the start of experimental narrative.

Giono, Jean (1895-1970). The most important of the group of rural writers that rose to prominence in the inter-war years. Giono was a staunch pacifist and his novels hark back to more ancient rhythms of life on the land.

Giraudoux, Jean (1882-1944). Playwright and novelist producing highly stylised works, written in impressionistic, sometimes hyperbolic, prose (*La France sentimentale*, 1932).

Glissant, Édouard (b. 1928). Writer whose theory of *antillanité* considers the special nature of modern Caribbean identity, emphasising its plurality.

Gracq, Julien (pseudonym of Louis Poirier, b. 1910). Novelist, poet and dramatist whose work, influenced by the Surrealists, depicts brooding heroes whose intensity often leads to disaster. Nominated for the Prix Goncourt in 1951 but refused it (*Le Rivage des Syrtes*, 1951).

Grainville, Patrick (b. 1947) Contemporary novelist best known for his innovative and original use of language (*Les Flamboyants*, 1974).

Green, Julien (1900-98). Catholic novelist and dramatist whose work explores violence, passion and fantasy in claustrophobic atmospheres (*Chaque homme dans sa nuit*, 1960).

Groult, Benoite (b. 1920). Writer of social realist novels and feminist tracts such as *Ainsi soit-elle* (1975).

Guattari, Félix (1930-92). Psychoanalyst and political activist who joined forces with philosopher Gilles Delueuze to produce the important text of cultural theory, *L'Anti-Oedipe: capitalisme et schizophrénie* (1972).

Guibert, Hervé (1955-91). One of the most prominent of the recent group of gay writers, noted for his work *À l'ami que ne m'a pas sauvé la vie* (1990). His writing is broadly autobiographical, exploring issues of gender, sexuality and disease with focus on the diseased body.

Hébert, Anne (1916-2001). Quebecois author and poet whose texts often treat themes of troubled maternity and the repressive, secretive nature of small communities (*Les Fous de Bassin*, 1982).

Hervé Bazin, Jean-Pierre (b. 1911). Linguistically playful novelist who portrays the inherent instability of family life through the figures of overbearing fathers and capricious mothers (*Au nom du fils*, 1960).

Houllebecq, Michel (b. 1958). His disturbing contemporary novels, portraying a disillusioned and depraved modern society, have made him a much talked-about recent author.

Huston, Nancy (b. 1953). Originally from Canada but now living in Paris, this contemporary novelist works on the interface between past and present, dreams and fantasies, with a particular interest in women's experience.

Hyvrard, Jeanne (b. 1945). Author of a series of texts exploring themes of women's identity, madness and language, through a return to myths of creation (*Les Prunes de Cythère*, 1995).

Ionesco, Eugène (1912-1994). Dramatist of the *théâtre de l'absurde*, originally from Romania, whose nightmarish plays include *La Cantatrice chauve* (1950), *La Leçon* (1951), and *Rhinocéros* (1960).

Irigaray, Luce (b. 1930). Feminist theorist and critic, Irigaray was expelled from Lacan's *École freudienne* for her subversive and original philosophical reading of the nature of female sexuality and identity. *Ce sexe qui n'est pas un* (1977) is one of her best-known works.

Jabès, Edmond (b. 1912). Poet and mystic whose work is often concerned with the Holocaust, he explores how to articulate truth through paradox (*Je bâtis ma demeure*, 1959).

Jaccottet, Philippe (b. 1925). Poet whose landscape poems show a Romantic yearning to reach some higher meaning (*Airs*, 1967).

Jacob, Max (1876-1944). Poet who described his verbally challenging and playful work as Cubist realism.

Jammes, Francis (1868-1938). Poet who celebrated the beauty and authenticity of the experience of nature (*L'Eglise habillée de feuilles*, 1986).

Japrisot, Sébastien (b. 1935). Contemporary novelist whose work plays with the conventions of the detective genre (*Piège pour Cendrillon*, 1965).

Klossowski, Pierre (1905-2001). Novelist and essayist influenced by Bataille and Sade.

Koltès, Bernard-Marie (1945-89). Playwright whose work, like Genet's, champions the criminal in order to explore new visions of reality (*Combat de nègres et de chiens*, 1983).

Kristeva, Julia (b. 1941). Literary critic and psychoanalyst whose work has focused, among other questions, on the complicated process of language acquisition and its link to creativity (*Soleil noir*, 1987) love (*Histoires d'amour*, 1983) and mothers (*Pouvoirs de l'horreur*, 1980).

Kristof, Agota (b. 1935). Her disturbing and often violent texts consider the meaninglessness of mankind's fate (*Le Grand Cahier*, 1986; *Hier*, 1993).

Lacan, Jacques (1901-81). Psychoanalyst whose complex re-readings of Freud founded a new school of analysis that has had far-reaching influence on psychotherapy, literary criticism and feminist thought.

Lainé, Pascal (b. 1942). A novelist who reworks literary models in order to destabilise conventional modes of thinking and representation. Best known for *La Dentellière* (1976) in which the image of women is in question.

Lambrichs, Louise (b. 1952). Contemporary novelist whose psychological thrillers explore the secrets hidden within a family, with particular interest in the trauma of losing children (*Le Jeu du roman*, 1995; *À ton image*, 1997).

Lanzmann, Claude (b. 1925). Film director whose documentary on the Holocaust, *Shoah* (1985), remains a powerful and moving testimony to this historical catastrophe.

Le Clezio, Jean-Marie (b. 1940). Novelist who offers a vision of the misfit alienated by modern society and whose lyrical portrayals of landscapes and nature contrast with his descriptions of the frenetic and indifferent city (*Désert*, 1980).

Leduc, Violette (1907-72). Lesbian novelist whose autobiography, *La Bâtarde* (1964) brought her, finally, a *succès de scandale*.

Leiris, Michel (1901-90). One of the later Surrealists whose experimental autobiography, *L'Âge d'homme* (1939), combined with innovation and originality the practices of collage, psychoanalytic free association and ethnographic description.

Levinas, Emmanuel (1906-95). Moral and theological philosopher (*Totalité et infini*, 1961).

Lyotard, Jean-François (b. 1924). Postmodernist critic whose theories aim to undermine belief in historical progress, the unity of the subject, consensus of meaning and all other totalising concepts (*La Condition postmoderne*, 1979).

Malraux, André (1901-70) Political novelist whose interest in the Far East led him to criticise Western bourgeois thought, proclaim the death of God, and denounce the meaninglessness of the human condition. *La Condition humaine* (1933), a classic novel in its own right, clearly influenced the Existentialist movement.

Mansour, Joyce (1928-86). Post-war Surrealist poet whose work contains strong elements of sado-masochism in its appeal for sexual liberation.

Maulpoix, Jean-Michel (b. 1952). Contemporary poet whose work aims to elucidate the origins and identity of what might be termed 'poetical', he produces difficult but beautiful work.

Mauriac, François (1885-1970). Novelist whose works explore the power and failures of the Catholic faith (*Le Baiser au lépreux*, 1922; *Thérèse Desqueyroux*, 1927).

Memmi, Albert (b. 1920). Tunisian author, one of the founders of Maghrebian literature, whose work traces the fluctuating identity of the Jewish community through time (*Le Scorpion*, 1969; *Le Désert*, 1977).

Merleau-Ponty, Maurice (1906-61). Philosopher of phenomenology, or the way we perceive and experience phenomena in the external world.

Michaux, Henri (1899-1984). Poet whose intensely emotional writing explores mental and bodily sensations and feelings, conveyed in a restless, staccato style (*Qui je fus*, 1927).

Modiano, Patrick (b. 1945). Novelist whose works explore loss of memory, often in the context of the traumas of World War Two (*Rue des Boutiques obscures*, 1978).

Montherlant, Henry-Marie-Joseph-Frédéric de (1896-1972). Dramatist in the classic bourgeois mould, his collaborationist themes got him into trouble after the Occupation.

Navarre, Yves (1940-94). Novelist, playwright and poet noted for his contribution to debates on homosexual rights and his provocative combination of lyricism and violence in the portrayal of homosexual relationships (*Le Jardin d'acclimatation*, 1980).

Ndiaye, Marie (b. 1967). Franco-Senegalese experimental writer who combines realism and fable.

Nizan, Paul (1905-40). Revolutionary Communist writer of socialist realist novels, of which *La Conspiration* (1938) is the most acclaimed.

Noailles, Anna de (1876-1933). Poet and novelist whose works chart strong emotional impulses towards religious purity or physical passion (*Les Éblouissements*, 1907; *La Nouvelle Espérance*, 1903).

Noël, Bernard (b. 1930). Poet and novelist whose dense poems, haunted by death and silence, struggle to find a language in which to express bodily existence.

Nothomb, Amélie (b. 1967). Contemporary author whose experimental novels explore the experience of writing, particularly in moments where it seeks to cohere an image of gender or authorial intent (*Hygiène de l'assassin*, 1992).

Ollier, Claude (b. 1922). One of the less well known *nouveaux romanciers* whose novels dismantle the narrative voice and its relation to the world beyond the text as well as the textual world of genre (*Mise en scène*, 1958).

Orlan (b. 1947). Performance artist best known for her recent controversial project of altering her appearance through a series of cosmetic surgery operations. The project, *Reincarnation of Saint Orlan* (1990-present day), is intended to question models of female beauty and to explore the interface of medicine, technology and identity.

Pagnol, Marcel (1895-1974). Novelist of the Midi who is now well known for the films by Claude Berri, *Jean de Florette* and *Manon des sources* (1986) adapted from his novel, *L'Eau des collines* (1963).

Pennac, Daniel (b. 1944). Exuberant contemporary novelist whose quirky texts have been both a commercial and critical success (*Au Bonheur des ogres*, 1985; *La petite marchande de prose*, 1989; *Comme un roman*, 1992).

Perec, Georges (1936-82). As a member of Oulipo, Perec placed mathematical constraints on his works in order to foster artistic creativity. The results are both original and spectacular (*La Vie mode d'emploie*, 1978; *La Disparition*, 1969).

Péret, Benjamin (1899-1959). One of the earliest Surrealist poets whose work attacked cultural oppression with a mixture of satire, burlesque and word-play.

Picasso, Pablo (1881-1973). Spanish-born painter whose work in his Cubist phase deeply influenced the Surrealists.

Pinget, Robert (b. 1919). One of the lesser known *nouveaux romanciers* whose work explored the nature of narrative voice and the process of story telling (*L'Inquisitoire*, 1962).

Ponge, Francis (1899-1988). Poet whose finely-wrought prose poems bring to life everyday objects while highlighting the process of perception (*Le Parti pris des choses*, 1942).

Prassinos, Gisèle (b. 1920). Poet and novelist whose early work was celebrated by the Surrealists (*Sauterelle arthritique*, 1935).

Prévert, Jacques (1900-77). Wonderfully accessible poet, known for his war poetry but also for his poems of everyday life that combine humour and visual impact (*Paroles*, 1946).

Proust, Marcel (1871-1922). The immense, lyrical, modernist work of art that is *À la recherche du temps perdu* (1913-27) remains a dominant feature of this century's literary landscape. Its themes – fictional autobiography, narrative experimentation, memory and sexuality – have shaped the modern novel.

Queffélec, Henri (b. 1910) Novelist influenced by existentialism whose protagonists must plumb the depths before approaching salvation (*Un royaume sous la mer*, 1958).

Queneau, Raymond (1903-76). A member of Oulipo along with Georges Perec, Queneau's anarchic humour finds its outlet in philosophically and linguistically sophisticated texts such as *Zazie dans le métro* (1959).

Quignard, Pascal (b. 1948). Novelist and essayists whose texts are often sophisticated and erudite (*Tous les matins du monde*, 1991).

Réda, Jacques (b. 1929). Poet whose work celebrates the fleeting, the intangible, and the insubstantial with wit and visual creativity. He has a particular interest in jazz and its rhythms (*Jouer le jeu*, 1985).

Redonnet, Marie (b. 1948). Contemporary novelist exploring the theme of memory through a series of narratives which mingle realism and fantasy (*Rose Mélie Rose* 1987).

Reverdy, Pierre (1889-1960). Pre-war poet whose fragmentary, typographically experimental poetry explored states of being (*Ardoises sur le toit*, 1918).

Ricardou, Jean (b. 1932). *Nouveau romancier* who went on to coin the term *nouveau nouveau roman* for his even more radically anti-representational work.

Robbe-Grillet, Alain (b. 1922). His *Pour un nouveau roman* (1963) redefined narrative purpose, in opposition to the committed literature of Sartre. His novels exemplify his theory, exploring the perceptions of the human mind (*La Jalousie*, 1957) and providing self-reflexive enquiries into the production of textual meaning (*Dans le labyrinthe*, 1959, *La Maison de rendez-vous*, 1965).

Rochefort, Christiane (b. 1917). Feminist writer who explores both the social condition of women (*Les Petits enfants du siècle*, 1961) and fantastic possibilities for their future (*Archaos*, 1972)

Roubaud, Jacques (b. 1932). Poet, mathematician and novelist, who was also a member of Oulipo. He is best known for his work of mourning *Quelque chose noir* (1986) written after the death of his second wife.

Roy, Gabrielle (1909-83). Montreal-born novelist whose work mixes past and present, urban myth and rural fantasy (*Bonheur d'occasion*, 1945).

Sagan, Françoise (b. 1935). Best-selling novelist whose work explores different manifestations of love and family values from a cynical, often bitter, perspective (*Bonjour Tristesse*, 1958).

Saint-Denys Garneau, Hector de (1912-43). Quebecquois poet whose collection, *Regards et jeux dans l'espace* (1937) heralded a literary renaissance in Quebec in the 1950s. His work focuses on the symbolic transposition of intense emotional states.

Saint-Exupéry, Antoine de (1900-44). Author of fiction and essays that offer poetic reflections on the nature of human experience. *Le Petit Prince* (1946) is a much-loved children's book satirising the adult world from a child's perspective.

Saint-John Perse (pseudonym of Marie René Auguste Alexis Saint-Léger, 1887-1975). Poet and diplomat born in Guadeloupe who won the Nobel prize for Literature in 1960 and whose poetry celebrates nature and the elements, rooting human identity and existence in a profoundly physical universe.

Sarraute, Nathalie (1900-99). One of the *nouveaux romanciers* whose texts challenge conventional plot and characterisation, focusing instead on the physical sensations and 'tropistic' movements that subtend human interaction (*Tropismes*, 1939, *Le Planétarium*, 1959).

Sarrazin, Albertine (1937-67). Algerian novelist whose brief life spent in and out of prison is reflected in a series of semi-autobiographical novels.

Sartre, Jean-Paul (1905-80). Philosopher, novelist and dramatist whose works explore different existentialist questions about the meaning of life, freedom and responsibility (*La Nausée*, 1938, *L'âge de raison*, 1945).

Saussure, Ferdinand de (1857-1913). Swiss linguistician whose theory of language as a self-contained system has been enormously influential in both literature and literary theory.

Schwarz-Bart, Simone (b. 1938). Guadeloupian novelist whose novels are concerned with the search for Caribbean cultural identity, and her husband, **André** (b. 1928), whose *Le Dernier des justes* (1959) is a meditation on the Jewish people's destiny of suffering.

Sebbar, Leïla (b. 1941). Novelist born in Algeria working in a variety of genres with particular interest in *beur* culture.

Senghor, Léopold Sédar (b. 1906). Poet and president of Senegal 1960-80, whose poetry explores aspects of black African history and identity and often incorporates stylistic devices from West African poetry.

Simenon, Georges (b. 1903). Author of the popular Maigret detective novels.

Simon, Claude (b. 1913). One of the *nouveaux romanciers* whose experimental fiction, resisting conventional plot development, sets out to question the reader's assumptions about time, history and narrative, he was awarded the Nobel Prize for Literature in 1985 (*Histoire*, 1967; *Les Géorgiques*, 1981).

Sollers, Philippe (pseudonym of Philippe Joyaux, b. 1936). Acclaimed experimental novelist (*Drame*, 1965) who co-founded the important Parisian literary reviews, *Tel Quel* and *L'Infini*.

Soupault, Philippe (1897-1990). Surrealist poet and novelist whose novels, written mainly in the present tense, are strikingly lyrical, dissolving the boundaries between poetry and prose.

Supervielle, Jules (1884-1960). Poet, novelist and dramatist whose work moves between fantasy, parable and myth, exploring the human urge to escape from loneliness and loss and exposing the impossibility of escape.

Tardieu, Jean (b. 1903). Poet and dramatist whose works are steeped in existential anxiety and concerned with the possibility of authentic expression.

Todorov, Tzvetan (b. 1939). Literary theorist who introduced the Russian Formalists to France.

Tournier, Michel (b. 1924). Novelist and short story writer whose provocative, often violent or shocking works consider issues of spirituality and morality whilst playing with the possibility of interpretation (*Vendredi ou les limbes du Pacifique*, 1967).

Tremblay, Michel (b. 1942). Canadian dramatist and novelist whose powerful works explore the alienation of the social underclasses through both strong characterisation and formal experimentation (*La Grosse Femme d'à côté est enceinte*, 1978).

Triolet, Elsa (1896-1970). Novelist whose work, concerned with the role of women in the Resistance movement, mirrored her own life.

Troyat, Henri (pseudonym of Lev Tarassov, b. 1911). Published a series of novel-cycles in the naturalistic style, e.g. *Les Héritiers de l'avenir* (1968-70).

Tzara, Tristan (1896-1963). Artist instrumental in launching Dadaism in 1916. His nihilistic work, crossing genre divides, challenges all social and literary conventions.

Valéry, Paul (1871-1945). Poet and essayist, famous not just for his stylish Symbolist poetry but also for his *Cahiers* – hundreds of notebooks in which he wrote fragments of theory, poetry and self-analysis (*Album de vers anciens*, 1920).

Velter, André (b. 1945). Poet whose works have a fascination with the lure of distant lands.

Vercors (pseudonym of Jean Bruller, 1902-91). Editor of the clandestine *Éditions de Minuit* of which his famous Resistance novel, *Le Silence de la mer*, was the first publication in 1942.

Vian, Boris (1920-59). Writer whose provocative, original works combine linguistic invention with fantasy and satire (*L'Écume des jours*, 1947).

Vilmorin, Louise de (1902-70). Wittily sophisticated poet and novelist whose light-hearted works are linguistically playful, she has fallen out of the public view of late *L'Heure maliciôse* (1967).

Vinaver, Michel (b. 1927). Novelist and playwright whose minimalist theatre dramatises the effect of wider political and cultural issues on daily existence, for example, his play on the Korean war, *Les Coréens* (1956).

Vivien, Renée (pseudonym of Pauline Tarn, 1877-1909). Poet credited with having 'launched' French lesbian writing at the start of the century.

Wiesel, Elie (b. 1928). Caught up irrevocably in the Holocaust, the sole survivor of his family, Wiesel's moving, highly regarded works continually reassess the causes and effects of Jewish persecution (*La Nuit*, 1958).

Wittig, Monique (b. 1935). Feminist and lesbian writer whose experimental texts deal with gendered issues of power and language (*Les Guerillères*, 1969).

Yacine, Kateb (1929-89). Novelist and playwright whose work has been concerned with the problems and possibilities for the development of Algerian cultural identity after the War of Independence (*Nedjma*, 1956).

Yourcenar, Marguerite (pseudonym of Marguerite de Crayencour, 1903-87). Poet, dramatist and critic, but best known for her historical novels that cover a range of eras and philosophical concerns with literature, politics and ideology (*Mémoires d'Hadrien*, 1951; *L'Oeuvre au noir*, 1968).

Index

Thody, Philip, 76
Tournier, Michel, 129-36

violence, 79-80, 130, 132-4
  in form of murders, 65, 75, 87-8,
    90-1, 93

in everyday life, 85, 99, 113, 117,
  118
  see also Holocaust and
    First/Second World War

White, Edmund, 20